"I first met Jim Walters in 1992. It was obvious that God's Word placed in an Air Force chapel in Thailand had a dramatic effect on his life. Jim has God's call in his life to proclaim God's love and His goodness through his preaching and his writings. *When Faith Takes Flight* contains the everyday, common principles that any believer can clearly understand and easily apply in our oftentimes tumultuous world. It is a most practical guide."

—Jerry Burden, Executive Director, The Gideons International

"You don't have to be a pilot to soar with this book. Jim Walters' vast flying experience has given him wonderful insight that will help you navigate through the clouds of life. *When Faith Takes Flight* will guide you to a gentle and safe landing in your spiritual journey. This book contains life-saving instructions for your personal safety!"

—Jack Pelon, General Manager, KPOF Radio, Denver, Colorado

"For over 30 years I have thought Jim Walters was one of the best preachers I know. After reading this book, I can now say he is one of the best writers I know. This book is brilliant! It is comprehensive yet simple. It takes the metaphor of an airplane and uses it to help us understand our relationship with Christ. As a believer, you will enjoy reading this and then find ways to share it with nonbelievers."

—Chris Liebrum, Baptist General Convention of Texas, Dallas, Texas

"Jim Walters stands in the pulpit of Bear Valley Church, takes the "spiritual stick" of people's lives and guides them through God's Word with as much reverence for Truth as for the laws of gravity. I commend this book to your pursuit of spiritual flight. This gifted pastor will instruct you to fly!"

—Dr. Bob Ryan, Mile High Baptist Association, Denver, Colorado

"Jim Walters attacks his faith and his mission to reveal God's truths to all who will listen and in particular his aviation colleagues and stick-buddies. His zest for life and flying has carried over from his fighter-pilot days in Southeast Asia to mentoring the young new aviators in training with the On Wings of Eagles Foundation, a faith-based nonprofit that provides aviation scholarships to at-risk and underprivileged youth."

—Bruce D. Oaster, Chairman and CEO, On Wings of Eagles Foundation, Inc., Lakewood, Colorado

"If you spend any time with Jim Walters, you will discover he has a passion for flying! While serving in the US Air Force in Thailand, Jim came to faith in Jesus Christ, and today the Lord is his greatest passion! Jim could explain the mysteries of flight in such simple and practical ways. Now he is using that same talent to share with you in a simple and practical way the mysteries of faith which will change your life for good—a change greater than the airplane made upon the world."

—Rodney Cavett, President, International Commission, Lewisville, Texas

"Whatever your stage in life, whether you are now searching for the Truth, or you are already a committed follower of Jesus Christ, you owe it to yourself to read this book. You will be glad you did! I know the author well. He is a man of integrity who can be trusted."

— Bill Tisdale, former missionary to the Philippines, Pastor and Evangelist

WHEN FAITH TAKES FLIGHT

Jim Walters

IPG

Intermedia Publishing Group

To Larry & Louise with Blessings Jim

WHEN FAITH TAKES FLIGHT

Published by:
Intermedia Publishing Group, Inc.
P.O. Box 2825
Peoria, Arizona 85380
www.intermediapub.com

ISBN 978-1-935529-16-3

Photo of Author courtesy of Randall Olsson Photography,
Golden, CO

When Faith Takes Flight

CONTENTS

ACKNOWLEDGMENTS

This work is dedicated to my wife, Connie, without whom I would be of little use to anyone, and to my daughters, Wendy and Bethie, who are a total delight to their father and mother.

Several men of God have had enormous impact on my life. These include (but are not limited to) Dale Cain, Jack Brown, Ben W. Mieth, Calvin Beach, Carlos Gruber, Rodney Cavett, Francisco Nuñez, Bill Tisdale, Tom Harris, Bill Grisham, JV Thomas, and Jimmy Smith.

Thanks also to the people of Bear Valley Church, for their constant encouragement to me in all of the Kingdom endeavors that we undertake.

Special thanks also to Co Baskin, Carol Vischer, and the 2009 Israel group, for their test-reading and feedback, as well as to LuAnn Turner, David Rupert, and Mary Ann Jeffreys for their excellent editing.

A special tribute is offered to the memory of Robert "Bob" Chamberlain. A pilot extraordinaire and a Christian gentleman, Bob mastered both manned flight and spiritual flight. His long and adventurous life was proof positive of the teachings presented in this book.

i

When Faith Takes Flight

INTRODUCTION
WHEN FAITH TAKES FLIGHT

The big airliner took off from LaGuardia Airport in New York and climbed westward over the Bronx. The weather was sunny, and passengers were enjoying the view of Manhattan. Suddenly the plane flew right through a flock of migrating geese. Normally, this would not be a tragedy, except for the geese, but in this rare case, each of the two engines on the big jet ingested birds. Both engines were ruined and incapable of being restarted. Without any thrust from those engines, the plane began to sink. The pilot, Captain Chesley Sullenberger, could still control the plane, but he did not have enough altitude to glide back to LaGuardia or to any other airport for that matter. Captain "Sully" would become a household name that day as he successfully ditched his plane into the Hudson River and all 155 people on board walked away (well, some swam away, but you get the idea).

What would you have done had you been on board Captain Sully's plane that fateful day over New York City? Do you understand enough about your own faith that you can call upon it on a moment's notice to strengthen and sustain you?

As the plane glided toward the Hudson, some people of faith might have offered a word of comfort to the other passengers or at least provided them with a picture of hope.

Other people may have been wishing they knew more about their own faith. At that moment, no one was thinking about politics or sports or how the market was doing. In those few moments, they were trying to sort out eternity and their potential place in it.

Waiting until an emergency like that is not a good plan for developing one's spiritual understanding. Today might be a better time to study and learn and gain confidence in your relationship with God, before a goose hits your engines.

Ever since the Wright brothers captured our attention, flying has become an integral part of our culture. We all enjoy flying stories, and we all have a flying story or two of our own to tell. Here is the gospel according to a flight instructor. I have taken many new student pilots up in a plane for a flying lesson. Usually, once they get a taste, they are hooked. Going up in an airplane and taking the controls is exhilarating. You can steer the plane anywhere you like, turning, swooping, soaring—the whole sky is yours. You feel totally alive and completely free of earthly constraints. To have your faith in God grow and "take flight" is even better. Once you figure out how to trust God for all the things you don't understand and you begin to cooperate with His grace working in your heart, your whole existence seems to swoop and soar into the wild blue yonder of God.

My father was a pilot. When I was in the second grade, he took me out of school for a whole day to fly with him as he delivered a plane for some minor repairs. While we waited, we walked all over a big airport and climbed in several planes. We visited the control tower and had lunch in the airport café. By the end of that day, I no longer wanted to be a cowboy or a fireman—my calling was to be a pilot! Years later, I had a personal encounter with my heavenly Father, and from that day forward, I was as excited about living the Christian life as I was about flying a plane.

Now, whenever I give a flying lesson, the student and I always walk around the plane, inspecting the wings, the control surfaces, and the engine. We discuss the fundamentals of flying, and I ask the first big question, "What actually makes an airplane fly?"

The surprising answer is—money. It takes tons of money to pay for the fuel and for the instructor who is crazy enough to go up in a plane with a student at the controls. However, the serious side of the discussion moves quickly through the theories and philosophies of flight to the practical. The big issue is *how do you actually fly this thing through the sky?* After all, everyone must obey gravity—it's the law!

So the issue for this book is *how do you actually live and walk and grow as a Christian?* Your "flight instructor" will not present much theory here. Rather, you'll see mostly practical steps and actions. Contained within are the first ten "pre-solo lessons" that will put spiritual lift under your wings and help you to get faith airborne. Each chapter will open up and explain a new topic, such as grace, faith, Bible, prayer, church, money, ministry, and love.

In each chapter, you will also find some learning exercises. As your instructor, I need to remind you to take the time to work through these exercises. Reviewing and reusing the information will make it stick. Some exercises will have you matching up information that you just read. Others will have you looking up Bible verses to gain new insights on your own.

At the end of each chapter, there's a quiz! But don't panic. It only has ten questions, and the answers follow. Grade yourself and figure out the answers to any questions you missed. This critical step will give you confidence that your faith is growing. How you score is not important; what's vital is that you review the missed questions. You want to exit each chapter knowing that you have grasped the material. Then you're ready to proceed!

Although this book is intended for personal study, each lesson contains Questions for Group Discussion at the end. The trick is for each person to read the chapter, work the exercises, and take the quiz *before* coming to the meeting. These open-ended questions will deepen your understanding and launch you into a higher walk with God.

THE FOUR FORCES OF FLIGHT

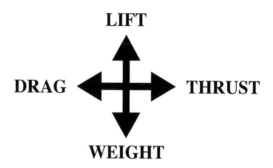

What really causes an airplane to fly? The answer is that four forces act upon an aircraft in flight, one acting up, one down, one forward, and one backward. *Lift* is the upward force generated by the wings, while the *weight* of the plane acts downward. The *thrust* of the engines propels the plane forward, while *drag* (think wind resistance) holds the plane back. Lift and thrust are positive forces for flight; weight and drag are negative forces.

In the same way, anyone who becomes a person of faith will also encounter positive and negative forces in his or her spiritual life. To help you understand these, a diagram like the one above, but showing four *spiritual* forces, will appear at the end of each lesson, to sum up the teaching of that chapter.

So let's climb aboard and get our faith airborne.

WHEN FAITH TAKES FLIGHT

CHAPTER ONE

GOD IS REAL AND CAN BE TRUSTED:
UP HERE, THE VIEW IS GREAT

You arrive at the airport, check your baggage, and make it through all the security checks. You reach the departure gate and learn that your flight will leave on time—that's good. You have a boarding pass and a favorite book, and you are ready to go. When they call your number, you will march right down the jet bridge and snuggle into your seat. After all, that's why you are here—you wanted to be somewhere else on the planet, and it was too far to drive.

Yet, in truth, most of us who fly on commercial airliners know almost nothing about how they actually work. We don't have a clue how to operate the controls. There is a maze of instruments and switches in the cockpit. We've heard that the air is thin and cold up at thirty thousand feet, and all kinds of complex processes must work just right in order for the flight to proceed safely. Yet we climb on planes all the time and travel places without a second thought.

For those who have a spiritual relationship with God, it works much the same way. We know almost nothing about God or the universe or how it all really works. We don't have a clue as to what the future holds, what heaven is really like, or whether angels are truly working on our behalf. In spite of this, we climb out of bed each day and live as people who have faith in an invisible God. At times, we sense His presence and His providence. Whether or not we are conscious of it, we enjoy His protection and His blessing. At times, we struggle to understand His will for us or His plans for our future. Still, we keep on trusting and cooperating with God if we have that faith relationship.

Not everyone finds it easy to believe. Many struggle with even the basic idea of God. One day I was conversing with a man, who, upon learning I was a pastor, let me know he was an atheist. He hadn't even told me his name yet, but right away he wanted me to know that he was not into God at all.

"Well, okay," I said, "That's interesting. I don't meet many real atheists. Would it be okay if I asked you a personal question?"

"Sure," he replied.

I took a breath and in a soft voice, asked him, "Of all the knowledge in the world, I mean all the knowledge on all the subjects in all the books and schools, how much would you say you possess? Would you say 10 percent, or maybe 5 percent?"

"Oh, not even 1 percent," he said, "Are you kidding? Maybe like 1/1000th of 1 percent."

I then asked, "That being the case, do you suppose it could be possible that God's existence is in the other 99.999 percent of knowledge that you haven't personally discovered?"

He thought for a moment, then said, "I suppose that's possible."

"Well, good," I replied. "You're not really an atheist.

You're an agnostic! And may I ask you one more question? Suppose God did reveal Himself to you; do you think you would resist Him or cooperate with Him?"

"Oh, I suppose I would cooperate with Him."

"Even better," I said, encouragingly. "You're not an agnostic either—actually, you're a seeker. You have no problem with God; you just haven't encountered Him yet."

He looked at me funny and said, "Don't ask me any more questions, okay?"

So I didn't, because I didn't want to push him. But, in truth, there are very few true hard-core atheists out there. Moreover, when I do encounter one, the other sincere question I like to ask the person is, "Would you tell me a little bit about your father?"

I ask that question because so far I have yet to meet an atheist who has not had a very negative experience with an earthly father. In some cases, it was a biological father, other times a stepfather, or even another male father figure. Often the negative experience was related to that person's either abusing him or abandoning him.

What is it about our experience with a father figure that is so powerful? How can that one relationship, if negative, turn a young life in a direction that is atheistic, or spiritually cynical? There is no simple answer to that question. One clue is that God chose to use this very metaphor, Father, to describe Himself. In other words, if our visible, earthly father was a disappointment, we (unfortunately) assign that attribute to our invisible, heavenly Father. Whereas in truth, our heavenly Father is incredibly better and more loving than even the best of earthly fathers.

The particular words in the Bible that describe God as our Father are worth noticing. Jesus is quoted addressing God as "Our Father" when He taught His disciples, and us, what we call the Lord's Prayer. Curiously, Jesus used an informal term as He prayed, saying "Abba" (literally, "Daddy"). His informality suggests intimacy and access. Linguists point out that the syllables of the word *Abba* are formed by two very basic sounds, "ah" and "bah," which became the sounds of the first two letters of many ancient Near Eastern languages. When babies utter their first "words," how often do those words sound like "ah-bah"? There's just something primordial about that sound, and Jesus chose it to describe our Father.

Show me a person whose earthly father loved her well. When that person hears that God loves her unconditionally and wants to provide her with eternal life, she is usually all ears! On the other hand, take a person whose dealings with an earthly father were negative: that person is likely to resist moving into a relationship with another father figure. One person actually said to me, "If your God is anything like my father, I don't want anything to do with that S*O*B." If your own personal experience with a father figure was negative, don't despair! You can overcome that painful loss, and you can gain an understanding of God (and establish a relationship with God) that isn't tainted by that experience. It will simply take a little more work on your part to learn how your heavenly Father is different from your earthly father. Within the Christian community, you can find mentors, pastors, even trained counselors, who can help you climb over these barriers. The danger here is, if you do not overcome this, you'll stay grounded and your faith will never take flight. You can win this battle.

Learning Exercise: Consider the following list of attributes that might be applied to a "negative" father: abusive, addictive, angry, absent, belittling, critical, dangerous, demeaning, discouraging, dishonest, foolish, foulmouthed, hateful, incestuous, mean, nasty, perfectionist, perverted, selfish, thoughtless, weak, zany.

That's kind of an A to Z list of human frailties and shortcomings. Do you recognize any of those from your own experience with an earthly father? The key here is to grasp that God is *not* like any of those words at all!

Here's another list: circle as many of the words as you like that describe what you *wish* your father had been like: authentic, brave, compassionate, consistent, devoted, faithful, gracious, honest, incomparable, loving, merciful, peaceful, truthful, and zealous. Add other traits not mentioned here.

_____

_____

Guess what? All of those terms describe our *heavenly* Father! His attributes are those and many more! Those who had a negative earthly father can find within a relationship with God the *Father they have always wanted.*

The yearning for a good Father might explain why 95 percent of all the human beings that have ever lived have believed in some kind of God. If you talk to the zoologists, the people who study animals, they will tell you that no animal anywhere on earth worships God, makes an altar, or prays. That's right: no animal anywhere worships God. (Yes, there is that little bug called the "praying mantis," but he only looks like he's praying!)

However, it you talk to the anthropologists, those who study human cultures, they will tell you that *every human culture* that has been studied worshipped something. Amazing! Perhaps they worshipped the sun, the moon, the river, the birds, or the corn. Or they just conjured up a deity of some kind so they could pray for help. It seems that we human creatures are simply hard-wired to perceive and respond to God, however limited our understanding of Him may be. It is normal, rational, and beneficial to believe in God!

The Bible has only a little to say about atheists. One passage, Psalm 14:1, says, "The fool has said in his heart, "There is no God.'" Is that a statement of denying any belief, or rather, a statement of rejection? In the Hebrew, the fool only says, "no God." That statement could be translated as disbelief or as rejection. Suppose you offered me coffee and I said, "No coffee." I'm not saying coffee doesn't exist; rather, I am just saying that I don't want any coffee right now. Often, the atheist isn't so much convinced of God's nonexistence as he is convinced that he just doesn't want any part of God right now, thank you. Declaring an atheistic position usually wards off people who wish to influence him toward faith. But honestly, to be a hard-core atheist, one would have to assert that 95 percent of all the people who have ever lived were deluded in their belief about the existence of a God. How much fun would it be to live in a world where you had to write off 95 percent of your fellow inhabitants as delusional?

There are also rational and philosophical reasons for believing in God. The seventeenth-century mathematician Blaise Pascal came up with a simple yet elegant theory that goes like this: The knowledge of God cannot be proved or disproved, because the concept of God is itself *outside* of our sphere of understanding. Therefore, each person is going to make a wager: either there is a God, or there is not. Place your bets! However, before you do, perhaps it would be wise to consider the consequences of your position. If you bet that there is a God, and it turns out that there is not, that's one kind of disappointment. If you bet against God's existence, and it turns out you are wrong, that God does exist, this is a tragedy of another magnitude. Anyone who buys into the idea of "Pascal's wager" will find it wise to side with the 95 percent of the world's population who say, "We think God exists."

Enough of philosophy—let's get practical. I could show you pictures of airplane wings and diagrams of lift vectors in order to prove that manned flight is possible. You already know this—you have personal experience flying in airplanes.

What if I said you could work out God's existence in your own life in a similar way, by personal experience? This has been the case for millions and millions of other people. It could be the case for you, too. "Taste and see that the LORD is good," is the invitation to you (Psalm 34:8).

So how do you try out God? You begin by trusting Him. You can give Him a chance. You simply open up your mind and heart and will to the idea that there is a God, and wait to see what happens. God *will* reveal Himself to you. He says in Jeremiah 29:13, "You will seek me and find me when you seek me with all your heart."

Since you are reading this book, chances are strong that you are at least open to the possibility of a spiritual relationship with God. It's like when you're racing down the runway in a plane, wishing you could fly. Just pull the stick back, and the plane will take off on its own!

You are not alone in your willingness to believe. Billions of people over thousands of years have believed in a divine creator, and in an afterlife. These are not just ordinary people either. Consider that most of history's brilliant composers, artists, and sculptors believed in God. (They were not always churchgoers, but they believed in and respected God.)

Here's a quiz: circle the names in the following group who were known to be atheists:

Alexander the Great	Napoleon	Constantine
Leonardo da Vinci	Michelangelo	Rembrandt
George Washington	Abraham Lincoln	Thomas Jefferson
Johann Sebastian Bach	Ludwig Von Beethoven	Frederic Handel
Albert Einstein	The Wright brothers	Isaac Newton
Joan of Arc	Florence Nightingale	Catherine the Great

The answer, of course, is "none of the above." All of these people in one way or another acknowledged that a divine power had set the universe in motion. To be fair, not all of these were Christians *per se*, or even theists (people who believe that God is active in our world today). Some would be best described as deists (people who believe that a Supreme Being created the world through natural means, rather than through miraculous intervention.) Deists acknowledge there is a God but are not inclined to pray, believe, go to church, or sing. They act as if God made the world and then gave it a shove out into space, without so much as a "good luck" nudge. (That might be like someone leaving an unlocked airplane at the airport with a note taped to the control wheel, saying "good luck.")

Did you know that not even one of the forty-four men elected president of the United States has been a professing atheist? (Some may have lived like they were atheists, but that's a subject for a different book!) Out of the one hundred men and women who serve in the United States Senate, currently ninety-nine of them profess a belief in God, and the other one waffles on the issue. (If you're curious about this, check out www.adherents.com/gov/congress_107.html.)

Learning Exercise: "Who Believes in God?"

See if you can match these terms to their descriptions:

1. Atheist

A - A person who is spiritually curious about God, and who desires a relationship with God but is not yet convinced.

2. Agnostic

B - One who believes that an intelligent designer created the universe and left a record of His work through religious writings, but who is no longer present and active in the affairs of the world.

3. Seeker

C - One who is convinced beyond any doubt that there is no God.

4. Deist

D - One who not only believes in an active God but lives in a spiritual relationship with God, prays and expects God to hear his or her prayers, and obeys and anticipates a reward for obedience.

5. Theist

E - A person who doesn't believe in God but acknowledges that God's existence might be real. They simply don't know for sure.

6. Believer

F - One who believes that God is active and present in the world, but who may or may not have any personal connection to God.

Answers:1C; 2E; 3A; 4B; 5F; 6D

The Bible says that out of all creation (nature), people alone are made "in the image of God" (Genesis 1:27). That might mean many things. One of the more obvious meanings is seen in the difference between plants, animals, and humans. Plants are alive in the sense that they have cells that take in food and digest it and reproduce more cells, but that's all that plants have: a body.

Animals have a body like plants, but also have a mind, a will, and emotions. The New Testament calls this a soul, (the Greek term is *psyche* from which we get "psychology"). This is not a soul in terms of religious usage (i.e., a lost soul that needs to be saved). No, the word here refers to a living-being soul that has a mind, will, and emotions, by which animals all exist on a plane of consciousness, which plants do not.

Still, their existence is significantly different than humans. For starters, humans have several things that most animals do not: opposable thumbs, year-round mating season, and a highly developed cerebral cortex. But even beyond that, human beings have spirit, which we could define as both a God-consciousness and a self-consciousness. That's really what sets human beings apart from every other creature on earth.

This spirit, this essence that is within every person, cannot be located anatomically or proved by medical science. Curiously, both the Old and New Testament words for "spirit" mean "wind," or "breath." They carry the idea of something not physical, something not made of matter, something too ethereal to be seen with the eye or grasped in the hand.

Ancient Hebrews thought the center of man's essence was down somewhere in his bowels, perhaps in his intestines. In modern times, we refer to this part of our being as "down in my heart." A recent book by a medical doctor, *The ESP Enigma*, by Diane Hennacy Powell, has some astounding news to report. The book says that modern medicine is now recognizing that both the heart and the intestines have a kind of primitive brain within their organs. The gut contains a neural network of 100 million neurons. While that is a small number compared to the human brain's neurons, it is still enough to be capable of sensing, recognizing, recalling, and transmitting a signal to the body. No wonder we hear people say, "I knew in my heart," or "my gut was telling me..." We actually can know stuff and hear stuff from our hearts and our guts. Often while flying, I've had a *gut feeling* to recheck the weather at the destination, only to discover that unexpected storms had moved into that area.

The true spirit of a person, that ability to be God-conscious and self-conscious, is something way more spiritual than anatomical. Mark Twain said, "Man is the only animal who blushes, or needs to." Man is the only creature who sins, then laments that sin, and repents of it, to find comfort from God. Only humans know the agony of being separated (by sin) from God, and only humans know the joy of being restored (by faith) to God.

In her book *The Lovely Ambition*, Mary Chase wrote about her father's faith:

> My father was not interested in trying to prove God's existence, which, he said, was impossible, and therefore, a foolish waste of time.

Or in defining Him, which had been attempted not very successfully through the centuries only by human beings like ourselves.

He simply staked all that he had, and was, on a tremendous gamble that God lived and moved among us and that His active concern for His world and for all His creatures was constant, invulnerable, and unfailing.

There's a plan you can use to put wings to your faith. Just stake all you have and are on the notion that God lives and moves among us and is actively concerned for the world. Guaranteed — this will turn your life into a spiritual adventure and carry you to a higher level. We call this "winging it," and there are few more exhilarating experiences.

THE FOUR FORCES OF BELIEF

CHILDLIKE FAITH

REJECTION   **RECEPTION**

SKEPTICISM

Just as lift, weight, thrust, and drag act upon an aircraft in flight, there are similar forces that act upon your spiritual flight. Childlike faith will give you a lift with God — it will pull your soul up to a higher spiritual level. Listen to the words of Jesus: "Unless you change and become like little children, you will never enter the kingdom of heaven" (Matthew 18:3). Curiously, Jesus never said that children must grow up to be adults to understand the things of heaven. No, Jesus said that adults must become like children to understand them!

Acting in the opposite direction (downward, so to speak) is another force: skepticism. Skepticism will hold you down; it will keep your spiritual life from soaring. Having honest doubts about God, or asking hard questions of God, is one thing (and not a bad thing). However, hostile skepticism of the things of God, along with scornful negativity? These forces will keep you grounded!

A second pair of opposing forces can be seen in conflict in another dimension. Within the human heart are two possible attitudes toward God: an open heart, or a closed one. An open heart is a receptive heart to God's workings. In John 1:12, the Bible says, "As many as received Him [Jesus], to them He gave the right to become children of God" (NASB). This verse makes receptivity sound like the thrust from a jet engine, pulling you forward in life.

On the other hand, a heart inclined toward rejection will produce opposite results. It will drag on your ability to move forward or upward with God. It was said of Jesus' birth in the nation of Israel, "He came unto his own, but his own received him not" (John 1:11 KJV). Oh, what cold, hard words "his own [people] received him not." How did their rejection serve them? It served them like an anchor, holding them back from any spiritual progress.

Chapter One Quiz

1. The primary metaphor the Bible uses for God is:
   a) God is like a dictator.
   b) God is like a father.
   c) God is like a judge.
   d) God is like a teacher.

2. According to anthropologists and zoologists, a common difference between people and animals is:
   a) only people use tools and communicate
   b) only people have opposable thumbs
   c) only people pray and worship
   d) only people can think and feel

3. Many of our Founding Fathers were deists who believed that:
   a) God did not exist at all
   b) God did create the world but is not now active in its daily affairs
   c) God did create the world and is readily involved in its daily affairs

4. Atheists believe that there might be a God, they just don't know or care either way.
   a) True
   b) False

5. The term *spirit* refers to our God-consciousness and our self-consciousness.
   a) True
   b) False

6. Blaise Pascal said that the best way to gamble on God's existence was to:
   a) live like there's no God and don't sweat it
   b) live like there's no God and pray you're not wrong
   c) live like there might be a God, because you have little to lose
   d) live like there might be a God, lest people think you are weird

7. It is possible to experience God by:
   a) understanding God with your mind
   b) pleasing God by your moral strength
   c) cooperating with God by trusting Him
   d) coercing God into doing your will through prayer

8. Jeremiah the prophet quotes God as saying, "If you seek me...
   a) you will not find me
   b) you will find me
   c) you will be rewarded
   d) you will be an idiot

9. According to the Bible, man is the only creature that:
    a) Thinks
    b) Sins
    c) Feels

10. One attitude that will retard your spiritual growth is:
    a) Curiosity
    b) Honest doubts
    c) Moral stumbles
    d) Skepticism

Questions for Group Discussion

Get to know others on the flight:

Describe your first experience in a plane. Was it a good or bad experience?

If you could fly anywhere in the world today, where would you go? Why would you make that selection?

Flying higher:

Describe your earthly father.

Describe your heavenly Father as you know Him now.

Are you one for whom trusting God is more difficult, or easier? Why do you think that is?

When and why did you first trust God?

Let your imagination take flight:

What's your spiritual flight plan? We don't get on a plane without knowing where we are going; we shouldn't take off on a spiritual flight without a destination in mind either.

Where would you like to go spiritually as you read this book?

Quiz answers: 1b, 2c, 3b, 4b, 5a, 6c, 7c, 8b, 9b, 10d

Chapter Two

Welcome to Earth:

Grounded on a Broken, Fallen Planet

The sun had just set over the mountains of northern New Mexico, when the plane flew over our ranch headquarters. I recognized the plane immediately, because three other pilots and I had rented it from a nearby airport and brought it to this remote airstrip to use for a month.

Seeing it in the air after sunset was shocking, because our airstrip had no light. In the mountains, once the sun disappears, it gets dark in a hurry. Another pilot and I jumped into pickup trucks and drove down to the airstrip. We parked our trucks at each end of the darkening strip and hoped the pilot in the air would understand our signal (the runway was between the truck lights). Alas, he did not. He made a series of poor decisions, creating what pilots call an *accident chain*. If any of the links in the chain had been broken, by just one good decision, there would have been no accident.

First off, he should not have been up there after sunset. Second, he could have flown to the nearby lighted airport; we would have driven there to meet him. Third, he missed our signal. Fourth, he didn't lower the flaps, in order to come in slowly. As he approached the ground, he didn't see the white color of our gravel strip—all he saw was green grass in the pasture, but he landed anyway. Finally, after touchdown, he didn't brake hard to a stop. Rather, he rolled and rolled, across the dark grass, until he hit the ditch! The plane nosed down into the ditch, and the propeller dug into the bank. Scratch one airplane. Fortunately, he and the passenger walked away unharmed.

Why did that happen? Here was a good pilot, well trained and experienced. Now he has an accident on his record, and the FAA will require him to do additional training. Insurance adjusters and maybe attorneys will enter the picture. His passenger friend may never want to fly again. All in all, it's a disaster. It's a bad thing that has happened to some people.

People often ask me, "Why do bad things happen to good people?" It's a fair question, but a tough one. There are several simple answers, and they are mostly wrong. When asked this question, I usually take a deep breath and respond slowly and carefully.

"First," I say, "Let us agree that no answer I can give you is going to be completely satisfactory to you. The library over at the theological seminary has a whole shelf of books on the topic of suffering, and none of them contains answers that would totally satisfy you. However, if you're willing to accept a few partial answers, answers that are like small pieces of a jigsaw puzzle, answers that will let you see bits and pieces of a larger picture, then perhaps you can get some relief on this subject."

The starting point is this: earth is a broken, fallen planet. It's a lousy, stinking, disease-ridden, war-rocked, poverty-infested, politically corrupt planet, but it's the only planet we have. Despite NASA's wildest dreams, we truly have no other place to go in our lifetime!

"There is a heaven, but this is not it," I often tell my congregation. "We are living on earth, and earth is no paradise." Once you accept this sad reality, once you really chew on it and choke it down, the reality of life on earth will make a lot more sense to you.

Everything is broken! Nothing works perfectly. No one lives perfectly; no one always gets it right, not even the animals. They all grow old, get sick, and die. Plants suffer from various diseases, some of which kill off entire crops and species. The weather is broken too—that's why tornados, hurricanes, droughts, and floods come. Marriages are broken to the point that only half of the new ones will survive. All around the world, parenting is broken, and families are dysfunctional. To say that we live on a broken, fallen planet is truly a self-evident truth. As Will Rogers might have said, "It's in all the newspapers."

Honestly, read any section of a newspaper. Crime, disease, tragedy, war, death—it's all there, usually on page one. "If it bleeds, it leads," says the journalist.

The second little piece of the big answer comes as a shocker to many people: God's agenda is not to turn earth into heaven. No, sorry to disappoint you, but that is not His plan for now. As Abraham Lincoln famously said, "The Almighty seems to have His own purposes." God has His reasons for the earth's continued broken state. According to the Bible, God does have an agenda, but it is not the one many people think it is. So what kind of God is He, anyway?

God is all-powerful, right? God is all-good, right? Yet

bad things happen to people. How can you reconcile those three ideas? Look at these three truths in the form of a logical argument:

1. God is all-good.

2. God is all-powerful.

3. Bad things happen to people.

Pick any two of the three truths, and you can make sense of it. Try to put all three together, and it just doesn't work. If God is all-good and all-powerful, then bad things should not happen. The human brain is like a pocket calculator that has seven digits in its little display window. If you input a problem where the answer would require nine digits, the thing just blinks at you with an error message.

That's what the human brain tends to do when confronted with this logical dilemma. The brain says, "It just doesn't add up," and the brain is correct. Then the brain goes *tilt*, like a pinball machine. This can create a real problem for some people, but it is not a problem for God. What to do? You'll just have to live with this dilemma, until you get to heaven. Accepting the reality of earth will give you some power to help you deal with it. Moreover, it's not going to change anytime soon, no matter who is elected to any political office, or how many bad people we lock up in prison, or what advances science and technology make in medicine. Trust me on this: earth is a broken place where sometimes your airplane ends up in a ditch on a dark night. Earth is a place where sin has created a separation between people and God. Deal with it.

Let's look at a basic theology of sin. The New Testament

has three different words for sin, each with its own word picture.

The first word is *sin*. It means "falling short of the mark," like an arrow fired by an archer toward a target that lands in the dirt far short of the mark. Actually the distance that it flies is irrelevant, and how far short of the mark isn't important either. What matters is, it fell short. I once watched a plane that had run out of gas try to glide to a landing at an airport on the west coast of Florida. The female pilot managed to glide across Tampa Bay, but she landed short of the airport. Instead of on the runway, she came down in the mudflats. She had handled her problem as well as she could and walked away uninjured, but she didn't quite make it to her goal. Such is life.

In this sense, everyone in the world has sinned. "All have sinned and fall short of the glory of God," says Romans 3:23. Everyone who's lived long enough to know right from wrong has at some point selected wrong over right. Congratulations. As part of the human race, you have sinned and fallen short of God's perfection.

The second word is *transgression*. The prefix *trans* usually means "across," and this is no exception. Transgression is "crossing the line," as in, you knew where the line was, and you slipped over it anyway. Think of the Ten Commandments. Here God drew a line in the sand, in just ten terse commands. A popular billboard sign of recent days asked, *What part of "Thou shall not" do you not understand?* Anytime you violate one of those laws, such as, when you tell a little white lie, you feel it in your conscience! You certainly know that you're not supposed to tell lies, but—boom—there it went, flying out between your lips. Congratulations! You have just transgressed a law of God.

The third word for sin is *iniquity*, a nasty sounding term. It means a moral twisting. Even today, when we say something is "twisted," we imply a dark context, a deviation of some kind. *Iniquity, inequity, inequality*: all are wicked-sounding words. This kind of sin is different from mere imperfection. This kind of sin twists God's truths; it violates them blatantly. "Woe to those who call evil good and good evil, who put darkness for light and light for darkness, who put bitter for sweet and sweet for bitter." (Isaiah 5:20.)

In the counterculture of the 1960s, it became pejorative to be a square. "He's an L-7," they would jeer, using their thumbs and forefingers to form a square. They may have targeted the term *square* because of the popular Cub Scout motto that said, "To be square." To be square meant to be honest and upright in all matters. Even today, a Boy Scout promises in his Scout oath to be "morally straight" in his lifestyle. Yet even the best Boy Scout will find his morals at least slightly twisted at some point. Congratulations, your iniquity is part of your humanity.

Here's a useful definition of sin that gets down to the heart of the matter: sin is the attitude that wishes God were dead. Oh, wow. Just think about that for a minute. Sin is the complete anti-God state of mind. If God were dead, then one could just do as one pleased, with no fear of consequences. If that mind-set ever took hold among the whole population, anarchy would soon reign. William Golding's classic novel, *Lord of the Flies*, depicted just such a scenario. Golding wrote about a group of schoolboys who end up shipwrecked on a deserted island. The land had sufficient resources to support them, but they were completely unable to govern themselves, resulting in predictable and disastrous results for all. Golding purposefully titled the book from the Old Testament words for Beelzebub, a title given to Satan, as "God of the flies."

I've seen pilots commit all three kinds of errors like these. In addition to the pilot who ran out of gas and landed *short of the mark*, I've been around pilots who flew into thunderstorms, *crossing a line* that they knew full well could be fatal (and sometimes it was). Others *twisted* the intended use of their planes, using them to smuggle drugs (often their careers ended abruptly).

So how did all this sin get into our world in the first place? According to the Bible, in the beginning, everything was fresh and green; there was no disease, no death, no wars, no poverty, no conflicts, and best of all, no sin. The whole earth operated pretty much the way we might ideally think it is supposed to operate.

Then people sinned, and everything changed. The consequences of those sins were ghastly and global. Once the spiritual DNA of the human race was corrupted, that fatal flaw spread to each of the following generations — like a pandemic. Every human being suffers from an inherited flaw: the tendency to sin. It is true that we commit sin both by acts of commission and by acts of omission (doing stuff that we should not do, and not doing stuff that we should do). A deeper truth is that *we are sinful*, even before we get around to doing or not doing stuff. We are corrupt by nature, and that is what makes the earth such a tragic place. Six billion people and all of them are sinners. Yikes!

One of our sinful tendencies is to think that we are in charge, and we want to tell God how to do His business (or we just won't believe in Him). Consider this parable about a "repentant God." Suppose that a bunch of people complain to God about the tragic situation on earth. They whine and moan about how awful it is that some children die of cancer, and they protest by telling God, "We will not worship a God who allows children to die of cancer." And suddenly, God sits up and pays attention.

God says, "You have got a point here. You're right!" Shazam! The world changes and suddenly no more children ever die of cancer. That would fix everything, wouldn't it? Now everyone would worship God, and there would be no more complaints or anger at God. Right? Wrong.

Hardly a week would go by until the complainers would return, saying, "But, God, there are also blind children. Do something. We can't worship the kind of God who would allow children to go through life blind." And God relents again. Shazam! The rules change, and all children have their sight returned. Now maybe the people would worship God.

Not a week would go by and the complainers would be back. "God, what about the crippled children?" The following week: "God, you must do something about famine and war and all diseases and poverty and old age and depression and death."

You get the picture, don't you? There would be no end to it. The people who complain today would complain every single day of their lives, until every single aspect of life was perfect. That perfection is what we call heaven. There is a heaven, friends, but this isn't it. Deal with this fact, and you'll help yourself to prepare for spiritual flight. It is not God's fault that the world is broken—it is our fault.

Truth be told, there's a lot of mystery to this issue. Don't let it get you bogged down.

Even the apostle Paul, the great interpreter of Jesus, who wrote half of the New Testament, put it this way: "We see through a glass, darkly" (1 Corinthians 13:12 KJV).

Final point: how could God create man and woman, give them free will to choose between good and evil, and then hold them responsible for their mistakes when they choose evil? Well, what's the alternative? God could create mankind and make them robots, so that they never sin? Hmm, not much *glory to God* there, and not much *fellowship with God* either. Creating robots is something like flying on autopilot— nothing could be more boring.

Maybe God could give them what appears to be free will, but secretly hardwire each and every creature to choose correctly every time, every day. That way, people could freely choose to glorify God and fellowship with Him. But wait, if they are hardwired, how much freedom is there really?

Or, try this: what if God truly gave them free will to choose and He set the consequences for wrong choices to be very harsh. Then He also provided, in advance, a provision for rescuing them from their bad choices. God's plan would be: to tear off a part of Himself, re-forming that part into a human being, walking among humans, teaching, showing, loving, guiding, and then…taking the punishment for them. The people would have free will to choose right or wrong. Eventually, they all would choose wrong, sooner or later, but not to worry: built into God's plan would be a God-operated mechanism for redemption, called grace. Now this is no parable—this is actually biblical truth about God's overall plan from the beginning.

Learning Exercise #1:

Psalm 32 gives a great summary of the devastation brought by sin and also of the blessings brought by confession. This psalm (song) was written by King David, the shepherd boy who became king. David did great things for God, but he also fell into deep sin. He knew both "the thrill of victory, and the agony of defeat." Read these verses from the New American Standard Bible and circle the three terms used for *sin* as they each appear in two places.

> [1] How blessed is he whose transgression is forgiven, whose sin is covered!

> [2] How blessed is the man to whom the Lord does not impute iniquity, and in whose spirit there is no deceit!

> [3] When I kept silent about my sin, my body wasted away through my groaning all day long.

> [4] For day and night Your hand was heavy upon me; my vitality was drained away as with the fever heat of summer.

> [5] I acknowledged my sin to You, and my iniquity I did not hide; I said, "I will confess my transgressions to the Lord"; and You forgave the guilt of my sin.

A. Verses 3 and 4 depict the consequences of sin on David's physical, emotional, and spiritual life. Underline those effects. (Have you ever felt any of these?)

B. What was the key action David took to find relief? (Have you ever done this?)

C. Verse 1 describes the end result of that key action (poets often begin with the end in mind). What three words in that verse describe the end state of David's sin?

D. In verse 2, "does not impute" is an accounting term that means "does not charge." How would we express that thought in contemporary language?

Learning Exercise #2:

Here is a basic theological summary of sin and redemption from sin, in only five verses.

The verses all come from the New Testament book of Romans, which is a general, broad-based summary of Christian theology. (The book could be called, "The Constitution of Christianity.")

Read each verse and circle what you see as the key words in each:

Romans 3:23 — For all have sinned and fall short of the glory of God.

Romans 5:8 — But God demonstrates his own love for us in this: While we were still sinners, Christ died for us.

Romans 6:23 — For the wages of sin is death, but the gift of God is eternal life in Christ Jesus our Lord.

Romans 8:1 — Therefore, there is now no condemnation for those who are in Christ Jesus.

Romans 10:9–10 — If you confess with your mouth, "Jesus is Lord," and believe in your heart that God raised him from the dead, you will be saved.

Learning Exercise #3:

The clearest passage in the Bible that outlines the process and the result of confession of sin is text from 1 John 1:8–10:

> If we claim to be without sin, we deceive ourselves and the truth is not in us. If we confess our sins, he is faithful and just and will forgive us our sins and purify us from all unrighteousness. If we claim we have not sinned, we make him out to be a liar and his word has no place in our lives.

a) What are we to say about our sin?

b) What happens if we ignore our sin, or claim not to have any sin?

c) How does God respond when He suddenly learns of all our sin?

d) How much of our sin can be forgiven by confession?

e) How much sin is there besides "all of our sin?"

THE FOUR FORCES OF SIN

GOD

FLESH **SPIRIT**

SATAN
(prince of this world)

What are we? Are we human creatures trying to have a spiritual experience? Or are we spiritual creatures having a human experience? Each of us, being created in the image of God, is comprised of body, soul, and spirit. God wants to lift us upward, to a higher plane of spiritual life. But our enemy in "the vertical realm," the devil, wants to pull us down.

James 4:4 says, "You adulterous people, don't you know that friendship with the world is hatred toward God? Anyone who chooses to be a friend of the world becomes an enemy of God." The world, in this context, refers to the secular, antigod culture within our world. Friendships within the antigod culture can add unnecessary weight to your spiritual "flight" through life.

In another book, Galatians, two lists delineate clearly the opposing forces of "flesh" and "spirit" as they pull us in opposite directions. This is the conflict as seen along a horizontal line. The spirit pulls us forward in our spiritual progress, but the flesh holds us back. Look at these two lists that set these forces in opposition. First, the forces that drag us backward:

> The acts of the sinful nature are obvious: sexual immorality, impurity and debauchery; idolatry and witchcraft; hatred, discord, jealousy, fits of rage, selfish ambition, dissensions, factions and envy; drunkenness, orgies, and the like. I warn you, as I did before, that those who live like this will not inherit the kingdom of God.
> (Galatians 5:19–21)

Then, in the following verses, Galatians 5:22–25, the forces that thrust us forward:

> But the fruit of the Spirit is love, joy, peace, patience, kindness, goodness, faithfulness, gentleness and self-control. Against such things there is no law. Those who belong to Christ Jesus have crucified the sinful nature with its passions and desires. Since we live by the Spirit, let us keep in step with the Spirit.

Chapter Two Quiz

1. The basic word *sin* in the Bible means:
   a) to make God really mad
   b) to blow it once and for all time, without remedy
   c) to fall short of God's standard
   d) to fail to do as well as other people

2. The word *transgression* in the Bible carries the idea of:
   a) doing wrong when you knew right from wrong
   b) crossing a line that God had drawn between right and wrong
   c) breaking one of God's laws
   d) all of the above

3. Because of the original sin of mankind, everything on earth, including nature, is broken.
   a) True
   b) False

4. The idea that a good God would allow bad things to happen to people is best seen as a:
   a) condemnation
   b) paradox
   c) dilemma
   d) refutation

5. The term *iniquity* is a word picture of:
   a) really making God mad
   b) entering into some bad activity
   c) a moral twisting of right and wrong
   d) inquiring about what is right and wrong

6. There remains a lot of mystery to the issue of sin and brokenness and evil on earth.
   a) True
   b) False

7. God knew in advance that if He gave mankind free will, they would soon choose poorly.
   a) True
   b) False

8. In Psalm 32, David teaches us that harboring unconfessed sin could result in physical illness.
   a) True
   b) False

9. The two parts of our being, spirit and flesh, will be at war with each other as long as we live.
   a) True
   b) False

10. The essential point to grasp concerning the presence of evil on earth is:
   a) God's agenda is to turn earth into heaven as soon as possible.
   b) God's agenda is about solving all of our problems for us.
   c) God's agenda is to show us how much we need His help to overcome our sin.
   d) God's agenda is to improve people to the point that we can overcome all evil on earth.

Questions for Group Discussion

Get to know others on the flight:

Have you watched someone go through hard times in ways you admire? Tell us what you admired about their responses and reactions. (Use made-up names to protect their identities.)

Why is it so easy to make wrong decisions when our circumstances are hard?

Flying higher:

If two parents could do everything just right, could their children grow up to be perfect?

Even if one's outward behavior is righteous, is it possible to have attitudes that would constitute sin against God?

What is the difference between being a sinner and sinning?

Have you ever committed a sin? When did you first realize you were a sinner?

Have you gone through times of suffering in your past? What did you learn or are you learning as you reflect on that season of life?

Did you question God's goodness at that time? Do you now?

Let your imagination take flight:

Imagine how God the Father felt as He watched Jesus suffer.

Imagine how God the Father feels as He watches you suffer.

Describe the heart of God as you see it today.

Quiz answers: 1c, 2d, 3a, 4b, 5c, 6a, 7a, 8a, 9a, 10c

CHAPTER THREE

AMAZING GRACE:

THE CROSS GIVES US POWER TO SOAR

The sleek ten-passenger corporate jet pulled up in front of the executive terminal, and shut down its engines. A pilot opened the door and extended the little steps to the ground. I watched all this, expecting to see a business tycoon step off the plane with a *Wall Street Journal* under his arm, but no—the first person off the plane was an eight-year-old girl wearing a head scarf and carrying a teddy bear. She was followed by a woman whom I suppose was her mother, and the two of them waved good-bye to the pilot as they stepped into a shuttle van marked Children's Hospital.

I had just witnessed another free ride given to a passenger with a serious medical condition who needed to travel for treatment. This particular plane offers its services through one of several Air Charity Network nonprofit groups around the USA.

The patients have no legal right to expect this service; no law exists that would mandate private aircraft to do this. Nor do the operators receive any reimbursement from the hospital or from the patients. This is one absolutely no-strings-attached offer. It is a classic picture of unmerited favor, a totally undeserved gift that can be either received or rejected. It is a picture of what believers call *grace*.

A long time ago, before I came to faith in Christ, one of my own student pilots attempted to share his Christian faith with me. "I can't explain exactly how it works," he said, "but the death of Christ on the cross, all those years ago, had something very important to do with your sins and with mine, and with the purpose of our lives on earth."

It hit me as an odd statement; it was something I had never really thought much about. Yet it stuck with me, and years later I realized he was absolutely correct. He hadn't explained it clearly, (he was only a student pilot, not a true flight instructor), but, still, he was right on point.

Jesus' death on the cross had everything to do with your sins and mine. It was God's way of rectifying *everything*. It was the central action required to fix anything that was broken. The impact of the cross was immediate and retroactive. "The curse of the law" (Galatians 3:13) was broken, which means that the payment for sin has been made. Wow! That means that the people who sinned, which would be all the people who have ever lived, no longer have to pay the price for their sins. Jesus Christ died to pay our debt! We owed a debt we couldn't pay, but He paid a debt He didn't owe. That, friends, is what we call *grace*.

This is the central story of the Bible: Christ, on the cross. The Old Testament stories all occurred before the cross, and they centered on a concept of law, as in the Law of Moses. The Law of Moses included the Ten Commandments, plus hundreds of other regulations.

As explained by the apostle Paul (looking back on the law from the New Testament), the law was like a schoolteacher.

Schoolteachers always have lesson plans that describe their teaching objectives, and so do flight instructors. Every time we go up with a student pilot and help him spend $100 of his hard-earned money on plane rental, we better have something very specific in mind that we hope to impart to the student. The Old Testament had even more focus.

In the case of the Old Testament Schoolteacher, the lesson plan had one simple message to say to the world: you blew it! In other words, God has a law, and no one has measured up to it. The New Testament says, "All have sinned and fall short of the glory of God" (Romans 3:23). All of the law was designed to say to people: you need help! You fall short of God's standard, you are subject to His wrath and judgment, and in your own power, you truly cannot overcome this dilemma. The law is as complex as the instrument panel of a Boeing 767, but its main teaching point is simple: you need help!

All of the stories in the Bible eventually point toward Christ. Written at different times, they say different things, but they are all about Him.

- The stories in the Old Testament say, "He is coming."
- The Gospel stories say, "He died on the cross."
- The book of Acts says, "He lives."
- The Epistles (letters) say, "He reigns."
- The Revelation says, "He's coming again."

Let's take a minute and look at the first two of those messages.

"He is coming" is the theme of all the prophecies in the Old Testament. Some of these refer to His first coming (when He came to die on the cross), and some refer to the second coming (when He will come to rule and reign). Jesus is not identified by name but rather by title—or should I say titles. There are a dozen titles for Jesus in the Old Testament, such as, "Ancient of Days," the "Prince of Peace," "Lily of the Valley," or "The Son of David."

"He died on the cross" is the theme of the four Gospels that open the New Testament. These books read like biographies of Jesus, but they are so much more than biographies. The term *gospel* comes from the old-English word *godspell*, which means "good news." At first glance, one would think that the hanging of Jesus on a cross would be bad news, but not so.

The early Christian preachers like Peter and Paul understood that this was no accident, no tragedy. This was, in fact, the culmination of all God's actions and words up to that time. When they preached "the gospel" in sermons that ended up in the New Testament, their outline would consistently follow these points:

1. Jesus came from God.
2. You killed Him.
3. God raised Him from the dead.
4. He's coming back someday.
5. Therefore, repent, believe, and confess.

Theologians have termed that outline of the gospel the *kerygma*, from the Greek word for "seed kernel." That outline is a seed from which grows every truth of the New Testament.

These five points of the gospel are essential to understand God's overall plan.

1. Jesus came from God, that is, He came from heaven. He is the God-man incarnate (in flesh form). Jesus wasn't a regular person who invented a new religion. Rather, He was God who came down from heaven to walk among humanity.

2. You killed Him, you being the entire human race; you caused Him to come and die, because everyone sinned. It was our sin that caused Jesus to have to come and do this. There's no need to blame the Romans or the Jews or whoever for the death of Christ. On one level, it was everyone's fault, but on a deeper level, it was totally God's idea from the beginning.

3. God raised Him from the dead. That's what we celebrate every Easter. The risen Jesus was seen first by His women friends, then by His male disciples, then by large crowds of people. So many people saw Him, or knew people who saw Him, that conversations about Jesus' resurrection swept over the country. Furthermore, tens of millions of people from every century and on every continent have testified how their faith in the power of Jesus' resurrection changed their lives. Millions of people telling the same story: our pasts are forgiven, our present lives have meaning, and our futures are secure. That's a significant witness to the reality of the risen Christ.

4. He's coming back. This time it won't be to die; it will be to reign. The first time, he came as the "suffering servant."

This time, it will be as "conquering Messiah."

5. We each need to repent, believe, and confess. These are three action words that call for specific responses by the hearers. Many preachers today still end their sermons with a call to action (often called an altar call) that involves people's repenting from sin, believing that Christ died for them, and confessing Him as their Savior. *Savior* means "one who saves you." Look closely at these three actions.

First, to *repent* means to "change the way you think." In other words, to make a mental and spiritual U-turn. Ask any wise pilot what he would do if he found himself unexpectedly flying into a big dark thunderstorm, and he'll say: I'd repent. Well, pilots don't use that word, but the action they would take is — they would make a very deliberate U-turn. Pilots call it the "life-saving 180-degree turn." They know that if they just flew into the edge of a big storm, making that U-turn quickly will fly them right back out of that storm. However, the longer one presses on into the belly of the storm, the longer it is going to take to get out of there.

The second action word, *believe*, means more than it appears to at first. In modern English, *believe* might mean just to give a simple head nod of agreement, to make an acknowledgement like, "sure I believe in God." Usually this mental assent is given with no more thought than, *Sure, I believe the home team will win the Super Bowl this year*. But in Bible terms, to *believe* means "to transfer one's trust," to give up whatever else that you have been trusting, to put aside whatever else on which you based your hope. It means to go "all in," as poker players say; to leap into the deep end of the pool, to absolutely pass the point of no return. That's believing! (Note: the next chapter will cover faith in detail.)

The third action word, *confess*, means simply "to say the same thing" that another says. That's right. In the case of confessing sin, God already knows about your sin, so nothing you say is going to surprise Him. So just say it. Agree with Him that your sin is sin.

God's response to your confession will be to give you grace. This word *grace* is about much more than saying a prayer just before a meal. Grace means "unmerited favor." It refers to the loving-kindness of God. God longs to reconcile people to Himself in such a way that will result in their giving Him the honor (the glory) for their salvation.

If people can save themselves through good works, or church membership, somehow tipping the scales in their favor, then they can claim some glory for themselves. But if people are trapped in sin and totally helpless, and are saved only because of God's actions, then only God will receive the glory. And that is precisely what He wants! When He saves by grace, He gets all the credit.

That's what grace is all about: Jesus coming down to earth, walking among men and women, teaching, explaining, demonstrating, and then ultimately sacrificing, all on our behalf.

For Jesus, this was an indescribable act of unselfish love. For us, it is the greatest undeserved gift we could ever receive. We are pardoned! From our point of view, we only did one thing: we received His free gift. If that's not "unmerited favor," please tell me what is!

One dark night in West Texas, I was heading back toward

our home base at Lubbock, when an unexpected fog set in all over West Texas. The weather at nearby airports wasn't any better, and we barely had enough fuel to go all the way to a good alternate airport. So I decided to make one attempt to land at home before making the long run to the alternate.

We set up for an approach, using the Instrument Landing System, following a very accurate radio signal that could take us down to two hundred feet above the runway. My problem was, the fog extended down to one hundred feet above the ground. The tower controller said that even the control tower cab was up in the fog. But the air was smooth, and we were able to "fly the beam" right down to the end of the runway, coming in very low yet still unable to see anything through the fog. We came all the way down to the minimum altitude, where the pilot must quickly decide to land (if the runway is in sight) or climb back up (if the runway is not in sight). My passengers were pretty quiet as we all peered into the gloom, hoping to see something and knowing we were very close to the ground. Just as I was about to give it up, there they were! The flashing strobe lights at the approach end of the runway pierced through the fog, and they showed us that we were right on course. We slipped down over those lights and then suddenly we could see the runway — right in front of us. That night, I said some extra prayers of thankfulness for those lights that burned through the fog. They shouldn't have worked for us, but they did anyway.

That's how grace is too — it shouldn't work, but it does anyway. One way to remember this is that G.R.A.C.E. spells "God's riches at Christ's expense." If you get this key point, you are well on the way to gaining altitude in your spiritual life. The fact that "heaven is a free gift" and that it cannot be earned or merited by good works is the one central truth of the New Testament that seems to separate those who experience the new birth and those who are confused or put off by it.

Once grace has been applied to your heart, you are said to be *justified,* in theological language. Justification is a contraction of the words "justice" and "satisfaction." To be justified means to have God's legal case against you (for your sin) be satisfied, i.e., case closed. As a play on words, the state of being *justified* is like a state that is *just as if I'd* never sinned. Once God's justice is satisfied, He is then free to show you His mercy.

Mercy is a lot like grace. It might be described as the "other side of the coin": one side is heads, the other tails, and together they make up one coin. Grace and mercy work like that. Try this on: "Grace is receiving something that you do not deserve (like salvation). Mercy is *not* receiving something that you do deserve (like punishment)."

My favorite illustration of grace is this: I go into my favorite steak restaurant and order up a big meal. They bring out the steak, and I wolf it down. Then comes the check, and I have no money. This would be a problem, except that I have a gift card, which the waiter accepts. Soon the bill is paid in full, all is well, and out the door I go.

Was this a free meal? It was free to me, but only because someone else had already paid. Heaven works just like that. Heaven is a free gift. You can't earn it. The only thing you can do is to receive the gift, as it is offered by Jesus Christ.

This message of grace is summarized in one verse, Romans 6:23: "The wages of sin is death, but the gift of God is eternal life in Christ Jesus our Lord."

Understand that the wages (the paycheck, the end result) of sin is death. Death in the Bible is symbolic language for separation from God and from heaven. Can you imagine waking up in the hereafter and discovering these realities:

1. There really is life after death!
2. There really is a heaven!
3. You don't get to be there.

That alone would be hell, wouldn't it? To discover, although too late, that the biblical story of salvation that the Christians had tried to share with you was, in fact, true. Forget the fires of hell that go on without end and the other descriptions the Bible has for being confined to a place of eternal punishment. Just the knowledge that there was an eternal life in heaven and you missed it would be in itself a horrible fate.

Why take that chance? If you are reading these words, the really good news of the Bible is: you still have time! If you are still alive, if you can fog a mirror, so to speak, you can open your heart and receive the grace of God. It is a gift for you, just for the asking. You receive it by simply believing the promise of God to give you grace. You open your heart to God by inviting Him to come in and rule your life from within.

How would you know that you have received grace? First, according to the Bible, there is a "peace of God that transcends all understanding" that will "guard your hearts and your minds in Christ Jesus" (Philippians 4:7). To be "in Christ" is to have received grace. Some of the common experiences of people who find themselves "in Christ," are these:

1. You experience a shift in your concept of God, from "He's out there somewhere" to "He's here with me." This is an indescribable but common experience for new believers. Perhaps it's like the difference between watching *Top Gun* on TV and actually flying an F-14. It's now real!

2. You will occasionally stumble and fall short. You will still continue to sin, but not as a lifestyle. The difference is that, now, something deep within you feels pain when you sin. There comes a growing sense that your actions grieve God. Some people call this "guilt gut" because it is almost physical; it feels like a weight down in one's bowels. *Without* grace, a human being can sin continually and feel nothing. *With* grace, you still sin, but it hurts. You will then know what to do — go and confess the sin to God.

3. Once you have grace, there is an increasing "peace with God." There is no sense of distance to God, or anger from God toward you. Rather, there is a feeling of God's presence and love. As author Brennan Manning once said, "We Christians ought to walk around with our jaws hanging down in amazement, in a state of total wonder and awe, in light of what God has done for us."

4. Persons who are "in Christ" still want to do good works, but not for the purpose of getting to heaven. Once they have received grace and peace with God, they rest assured that

the whole heaven-versus-hell issue has been settled. Their motivation to do good works is now "because I *am* going to heaven" rather than "I *hope* to do good and thus earn my way to heaven." There is no longer any pressure to be *good enough for God*. A person's good works flow out of gratitude, rather than out of fear or guilt.

5. Guilt over past sin begins to fade away. Although it may resurface, it never has the power that it had before grace. People who have experienced grace *know* that their sins are forgiven, even if they do not always *feel* that way. That includes *all* their sins, past, present, and even the ones they haven't gotten around to yet. Some people think if they really believed that all of their sins, including future ones, were forgiven, that would be a license to run wild. Not at all. Instead, this sense of total forgiveness motivates a person to want to avoid sin at all cost!

So, in conclusion, can you see that *grace* is the key to experiencing God in your life? With grace, your walk with Christ becomes a relationship, not just a religion. Religion, with all its rules, all its dos and don'ts, can be really dry. A grace-based relationship with Christ is an adventure!

What do you say when you receive a gift? "Oh, you shouldn't have." Or, "Oh, I couldn't accept this gift." Saying that is silly. How about saying, "Wow, thanks! This is a great gift, and I deeply appreciate your thinking of me and giving it to me." You freely gave. I freely receive. Yes, this is humbling, but humility can be a good thing. James 4:6 says, "God opposes the proud but gives grace to the humble." Sometimes God seems to go out of His way to humble us, but it's not because He's mean. Rather, He wants to lead us to a position where we need grace.

I remember the day this principle became a reality for me, while I was an instructor pilot in the Air Force. It was a prideful existence: they would give me a jet plane, a student pilot, and a credit card, and say, "Be back Friday."

Our flying school would graduate a class of cadets every so often, and we instructors had to march in the big parade of troops. On one occasion, I volunteered to serve as a driver in the motorcade, where I would use a blue Rambler station wagon to deliver a VIP to the front of the reviewing stand. On this (dark) day, my Rambler was a ramblin' wreck, and my passenger was the wing commander's wife (think, First Lady of the whole base).

I picked her up at her home, and we joined in the line of Air Force blue cars cruising slowly across the tarmac. Because the back seat of this old heap didn't look clean, the First Lady had opted to ride shotgun (a small detail that is crucial to this story). The car ahead of me pulled up in front of the grandstand, and three high-ranking officers hopped out. That car moved ahead, so I pulled up in front of the crowd and stopped. The First Lady did not hop out. She just turned and looked at me. A light came on in my head: *she needs someone to open her door for her. Aha! I can do that.*

Quick as a flash, I released my shoulder belt, threw the door open, and stepped out onto the concrete ramp. I turned to my left, to walk behind the car, and noticed that the car was now moving ahead — on its own! I had left the thing in Drive. "Oh God, help me!"

I spun back around as the car cruised by my left shoulder.

I ran up into a position where I could leap into the moving car. But just as I leaped, the left rear tire ran over my right foot, pinning it to the ground. I did a face plant on the cement. My hat and my sunglasses went flying off. The car was still moving, picking up speed.

I leaped up and tried to catch up to the moving car. Running left and looking right, I caught up to the open door. Just as I was in position to leap again, one of the officers from the preceding car ran out to help, and we collided. I went down again; fortunately, he did not.

Again I was up and running. Ahead of the car there was a formation of troops standing at attention, but now they broke ranks and spread open for the approaching car. It was like Moses charging toward the Red Sea. I was almost in position to make another leap. What I didn't know was that the First Lady had released her seat belt and was sliding across the bench. Just as I leaped toward the open door, she hit the brakes. I smacked into the end of the door and went down a third time. Down for the count.

The car stopped; I lay face down, eating concrete. Waves of laughter poured down from the grandstand. It was the most exciting moment at any graduation parade in the history of Reese Air Force Base. All the people loved it. The commander's wife loved it; she was laughing so hard she was in tears. I hated it.

I who had been the proud jet pilot was now the Fool of the Year. *Why me, O God?* I cried. *Why would you let this happen to me?* I lay on the ground like a wounded insect, knowing I would never hear the end of this.

Ah, Grasshopper, the small still voice seemed to say, *pride cometh before the fall.* And when we're in a humble state, then God gives grace to us all.

The next chapter will explain how to put your total faith in Christ, both for the purpose of obtaining grace, and for walking in grace over a lifetime. First, take some time to work these exercises below:

Learning Exercise: (Look back at the text as needed)

1. Fill in the blanks that spell G.R.A.C.E.

G_____ R_____ A_____ C_____ E_____

2. Describe the "seed kernel" of the gospel.

Jesus came _____ _____. (He is God in the flesh)

You _____ _____. (because of your sinfulness)

God _____ Him from the dead.
(that's what we celebrate on Easter)

He's _____ _____! (and maybe very soon)

So _____, _____, and _____.

3. Can you pinpoint a time when grace became more than a word to you? Even if you grew up in church, and cannot recall a specific date, have you arrived at a place where you realized that you could not, in any way, shape, or form, save yourself?

If you cannot do that, why not say a simple prayer that admits to God that you know you are a sinner, that you know you are helpless to save yourself from sin, and that you want to receive His grace into your life, right this second! Then, pray once more, saying, "Thank You, Lord, for dying on the cross for me. Thank You for Your grace toward me."

Did you make this commitment to God today? If so, I would love to hear from you. Really—you can email me at jim@whenfaithtakesflight.com.

THE FOUR FORCES OF GRACE

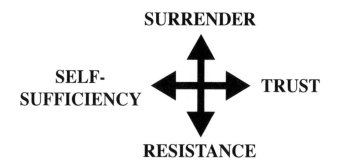

SURRENDER

SELF-SUFFICIENCY ← → **TRUST**

RESISTANCE

Would you like to receive God's grace into your life? Get down on your knees! No persons stand taller than when they are on their knees before God. "Humble yourselves before the Lord, and he will lift you up" (James 4:10). Stop trying to figure God out, and simply surrender to Him.

Abandon your self-sufficiency in matters of morals and faith. Place your trust in God, and He will propel you forward as if you have a jet engine strapped to your back. When the Apostle Paul was struggling with questions he couldn't answer, he heard this from God: "My grace is sufficient for you, for my power is made perfect in weakness." Paul then said, "I will boast all the more gladly about my weaknesses, so that Christ's power may rest on me." (2 Corinthians 12:9)

Chapter Three Quiz

1. The word *repent* literally means:
   a) to feel sorry for your sin
   b) to promise never to do it again
   c) to change the way you think

2. To "repent from sin" would mean:
   a) to admit that something is sin, which you didn't think was sin
   b) to willfully turn away from that sin
   c) to endeavor to not continue that sin
   d) all of the above

3. To "believe in God" in Bible terms means:
   a) not to disagree with God
   b) to intellectually assent to the idea of God
   c) to commit one's trust to God

4. To "confess" in Bible terms means:
   a) to take responsibility for one's shortcomings
   b) to make a profession, or a statement, of faith
   c) to agree with what God says about something
   d) all of the above

5. The essence of grace is:
   a) receiving from God something you do not deserve
   b) being blessed by God for your good efforts
   c) being "in" with God through church membership

6. To receive the grace of God, the indispensible action is:
   a) saying a prayer
   b) joining a church
   c) transferring your trust

7. A strong indicator that a person really has received grace is that although they still fall into sin, now sin hurts!
   a) True
   b) False

8. The big single point of the Old Testament "law" is:
   a) to set out the steps by which persons earn their way to heaven
   b) to delineate right from wrong and show which sins are fatal
   c) to show that no one measures up to God's standards

9. A person who is "in Christ" still wants to do good works:
   a) out of gratitude for grace received
   b) in hopes of obtaining forgiveness
   c) for the salvation of their loved ones

10. The human virtue most associated with grace would be:
   a) confidence
   b) chastity
   c) humility

Questions for Group Discussion

Get to know others on the flight:

Have you ever received a gift you knew you didn't deserve? How did you respond?

Have you ever turned down a gift and later regretted it? Why did you turn it away?

Flying higher:

Have you ever received a reprieve from a punishment you knew you deserved?

Do you still struggle with the concept that your good works won't get you to heaven?

Does the idea of heaven "as a free gift" make grace appear to come cheap? Why or why not?

Let your imagination take flight:

What would be a sacrificial gift you would like to give someone you love? Be creative.

Quiz answers: 1c, 2d, 3c, 4d, 5a, 6c, 7a, 8c, 9a, 10c

Chapter Four

Saved by Faith:

Wheels Up and on the Way

Imagine yourself flying a small plane through blue skies on a calm day. It isn't that much different than driving your car down the interstate, except that you don't have other planes so close to you. It's just you and the blue sky. There's a great sense of freedom, since you are not confined by white stripes to a narrow lane or even by pavement. You can turn and go anywhere you like, and even climb higher or descend lower, if that pleases you.

As long as the skies are blue, the actual work of flying a plane is a snap. You can see the ground, you can tell where you are by the passing landmarks, and you can tell if your wings are level just by looking out the window. This kind of flying is pure fun!

However, if your plane flies into a cloud, everything changes. The second the plane slips into the gray mass, visibility goes to zero. You can't see a thing beyond the windshield—it's as if you are flying inside a jug of milk. No sky, no ground, and no horizon. Those were your references to know if your wings were level or not. Also, since the human brain depends on visual clues for orientation, it quickly becomes confused about which way is up. It's hard to keep the wings level if you don't know which way is up!

We also depend on our inner ear's delicate mechanisms — little canals with fluid in them. These help us to keep our balance while walking down the street (or swinging from a trapeze.) But this inner-ear balancing system only works as long as it is backed up by visual references.

The bottom line? It is simply impossible to maintain any sense of orientation while flying in the clouds. Once the plane slips into a slight turn, or a gentle climb, those inner-ear fluid sensors will be telling you one thing, but reality will be quite another! For this reason, every airplane has a set of instruments right in front of the pilot that describe the plane's orientation, or attitude, in terms of pitch (up/down), bank (left/right) and yaw (flying straight or skidding to one side.)

For pilots, learning to trust the instruments over the inner-ear sensations is the ultimate act of faith. This kind of faith involves trusting in a system that cannot be seen or verified by bodily means. If my instruments tell me I'm turning, even though my body tells me I'm not turning, I must trust the instruments and adjust the controls. At first, this is hard to learn, as it goes against everything your body tells you is true, but it does get easier over time. I've spent enough hours flying in the clouds that it's no big deal anymore. You might say, when it comes to instrument flying, my faith in those instruments is solid.

More than three decades ago at 4:00 p.m. on a Saturday afternoon, I stood in front of a church and recited wedding vows, while holding the hands of my beautiful bride, Connie. Right after we left the church, we drove to a private airport, where she took her first airplane flight with me at the controls.

A friend had lent me his plane as a wedding gift, and we were off on a honeymoon trip. The weather was drizzly, and the clouds were low. We had barely lifted off, when we slipped into thick clouds and I turned my trust to those little instruments that tell which way is up. But my trust in the instruments was nothing compared to Connie's trust in me. She had no idea how those instruments worked, but she had faith in her pilot. Her belief was so solid that she took a long nap while I guided the plane through hundreds of miles of clouds and we arrived safely at our destination. I had hoped to impress her with my flying skill, but honestly, I was more impressed that she was so confident that she could take a nap. Now that's an exercise of faith, if I ever saw one!

These days when I am talking to someone about faith, I'll mention that I am a pilot and tell a flying story or two. Then I'll stop and ask him point-blank: "Do you really believe I'm a pilot?" To which he'll always reply, "Sure I do; why wouldn't I believe that?"

Quickly, I pull out a set of airplane keys from my pocket and say, "Okay, let's go for a ride. Let's see if you truly have faith in me as a pilot." The man will react one of two ways. Some people are eager, "Yeah, let's go flying." Others are like, "Uh, well, I don't know about that. I'm not so big on flying with strangers." Aha! Some people will say they believe, but their actions reveal their faith to be lacking and insufficient.

The simple truth is: Jesus is inviting you to go for a spiritual flight with Him! So the question is not, "Do you believe in Jesus?" but rather, "Are you ready to climb into the plane with Him?" You hear the clinking of the keys in your deepest heart. "Come fly with me," He says.

Do you recall a bumper sticker that said, "God is my copilot?" What a stupid bumper sticker! God is nobody's copilot, and we are not even His copilot. God does not need a copilot. Or a navigator, for that matter. As Max Lucado famously said, "We are just lucky to be on board and get peanuts!"

People ask me, "What does God really want from me?" Trust! That's what He wants. He wants you to trust Him as if He were the pilot of your life. Absolutely risk it all on His claims and promises. You put your life in His hands and go forth with Him at the controls. You transfer to Him the responsibility to save your soul for eternity, and you give to Him the control of the direction of the rest of your life. This is what is called *saving faith*.

It is faith that saves us from the penalty of sin (which is spiritual death and hell). Saving faith is what applies grace to our lives. Saving faith is what applies the work of Christ on the cross, to our personal account. When we place our faith in Christ's death to save us from our sinfulness, the blood of Jesus covers our sin. The blood is the payment for our debt. Jesus' last words on the cross were, "It is finished" (John 19:30).

In the Greek New Testament, the word for "finished" is *tutelestai*, which means, "It is paid in full." It's the very word that storekeepers marked on an invoice to show the debt was cleared. Through saving faith, the blood of Jesus is applied to our account and our debt of guilt is *paid in full*. We are saved from the penalty that we so richly deserved. That's why it's called *saving faith.*

Let's make sure you really understand this. How many of the following statements truly describe *saving faith?*

1. Faith is just having faith in faith. (Is this saving faith?)
   Circle one: Yes No

2. Faith simply believes that everything will turn out fine in the end. Yes No

3. Faith is a mental assent (agreement) to the notion that God exists. Yes No

4. Faith is the confidence that I have lived a life that's good enough. Yes No

5. Faith is totally trusting that God will do what He says He will do. Yes No

Hopefully, you understand that only definition number 5 represents true saving faith. In the New Testament, the word *faith* refers to a transfer of trust from self-worth and self-righteousness (as well as from good deeds and church membership) to God. Faith specifically trusts that God is who He says He is, and that God will do what He says He will do. It's something like taking a nap while the pilot is flying through the clouds.

God is a promise-making God, and the Bible is full of His promises. Someone counted a total 5,678 promises from Genesis to Revelation. Many of God's promises assert that faith is the operative action that is required of us. This is what makes New Testament Christianity more of a relationship than a religion. The life of faith is not so much about rules, regulations, and religious activity as it is about abiding in hope, and resting in faith, that God will keep His promises. This truth is absolutely liberating to the soul. The core of this relationship is trust; the outcome of the relationship is a new kind of life that honors God through worship, discipleship, spiritual growth, and moral behaviors.

Back to the promises of God: these promises usually are recognizable because of their "if-then" structure. "If you do this... God will do that." These two parts of a promise are called a "condition" and a "benefit." When you meet the condition, you receive the benefit. Second Chronicles 7:14 is a classic example of such a promise:

> If my people, who are called by my name, will humble
> themselves and pray and seek my face and turn from their
> wicked ways, then will I hear from heaven and will forgive
> their sin and will heal their land.

You can see the "if" at the beginning and the "then" that marks the transition. Let's break this promise into pieces:

Whom did God address this to? _____, who are called by _____.

And what do these people need to do to meet the condition?
    a) _____ themselves, and
    b) _____.
    c) Seek _____
    d) And turn from their _____ _____,
What does God promise to do on their behalf?
    a) I will _____ from _____,
    b) I will _____ their sin,
    c) I will _____ their land.

Many times the condition and benefit identifiers are not so obvious, but they are there nonetheless. Consider the most famous verse of the Bible (which, by the way, is a good one-verse summary of the Bible), John 3:16:

> God so loved the world that he gave his one and only Son, that whoever believes in him shall not perish but have eternal life.

Identify the condition in this promise:

"that whoever _____ in him…"

Identify the benefit of the promise:

"shall…have _____ _____."

Let's do one more, and this one is even more subtle: Ephesians 2:8–10:

> [8] It is by grace you have been saved, through faith —
> and this not from yourselves, it is the gift of God —
>
> [9] not by works, so that no one can boast.
>
> [10] For we are God's workmanship,
> created in Christ Jesus to do good works,
> which God prepared in advance for us to do.

Identify the condition in verse 8: "through _____"
(your part is to have this).

Identify the benefit in verse 8: "by _____ you have _____
_____."

Can you grasp what an amazing insight this is? When
you bring the faith, God brings the grace, and the result is:
you have been saved. Note that "have been saved" is a past-
tense verb. It denotes "completed action," something that
has been, shall we say, "Paid in full."

Verse 9 makes it even clearer. It says in plain language
that it "is not by works, so that no one can boast." Why is it
that so many people go through life thinking that the way
to heaven is to live a good life, to do the best you can do to
please God with your works? No! The Bible says it cannot be
done.

Verse 10 explains it even more. We are "God's
workmanship." Our salvation comes from *His* efforts, not
from our own. All we can do is transfer our trust to Him,
receive His grace, and accept His Word as a promise. This
action is often called "accepting Christ," and it is a one-time
expression of faith. Most people can pinpoint the time when
they made this commitment, to accept His gift. However,
people who grew up in church and have grasped this truth
for as long as they can remember may not be able to pinpoint
a date or a place. Still, they are quite certain that at some point
they did in fact *transfer their trust* and received His grace.
That's what counts!

Enough about saving faith—let's talk about *walking* faith.

Saving faith is what gets you to heaven. But entering this faith-based relationship with God (by His grace) is not the end of the faith experience. No, this is the beginning of the faith experience. From this time forward, all of your journey with God will be marked by the experience of "walking" in faith. Colossians 2:6–7 says,

> So then, just as you received Christ Jesus as Lord [by faith],
> continue to live in him [by faith], rooted and built up in
> him, strengthened in the faith as you were taught, and
> overflowing with thankfulness.

It is clear that God wants us to *continue* trusting Him while we journey forward in this life. Just as we were saved by faith, we walk by faith, and we grow by faith. And all this time, we don't get to see God with our eyes (rats!). However, 1 Peter 1:6–8 explains what God is up to:

> In this you greatly rejoice, though now for a little while
> you may have had to suffer grief in all kinds of trials. These
> have come so that your faith—of greater worth than gold,
> which perishes even though refined by fire—may be proved
> genuine and may result in praise, glory and honor when
> Jesus Christ is revealed. Though you have not seen him,
> you love him; and even though you do not see him now,
> you believe in him and are filled with an inexpressible and
> glorious joy.

God is acting like a refiner of gold—He's putting us through His fires, to purify us. Here is how gold refining worked in ancient days: the refiner built a hot fire, set an iron bucket on the coals, and poured in the gold nuggets. They quickly melted and turned to a liquid that could be stirred with an iron rod. (Gold melts at a much lower temperature than iron.) Soon the bucket contained a soup consisting of two elements: pure gold and the dross, or waste, found in gold nuggets. But the dross minerals are lighter than the pure gold. As the liquid heats up, the dross floats to the top. The refiner then scraps off the dross, leaving only liquid gold, which creates a mirror effect. When the gold is fully pure, the refiner can peer down into the bucket and actually see a reflection of his own face.

Now there's a life illustration if I ever saw one: God puts us in the fire of testing, heats us up through life's trials and tribulations, and stirs us until He looks at us and sees a reflection of His own character. Wow! Read the passage in 1 Peter again, and now you can see why he says that even though we don't see Him, and even though we are in trials, we can be "filled with an inexpressible and glorious joy" at being in a faith-based relationship with God.

The most famous chapter in the book of Hebrews is chapter 11 (but it is not about bankruptcy laws). Rather, it is a "hall of fame of the faithful." All of the people mentioned in this chapter were heroes of faith. Not all of them were successful in their endeavors (some were eaten by lions; others were killed by the sword), but the Bible says, "all these people were still living by faith when they died" (v. 13). And verse 6 says, "Without faith, it is impossible to please God." The verse explains that this is so "because anyone who comes to him must believe that he exists and that he rewards those who earnestly seek him."

That's good news. It promises that when we seek God through faith, when we seek help, answers, guidance, provision, and timing...then He rewards us! Human nature says, "I won't believe it until I see it." Faith says, "I won't see it until I believe it." Faith says that believing (the "seeking by faith") comes first, and then the seeing (the reward) comes second. The first verse of Hebrews 11 gives a great definition of faith: "Now faith is being sure of what we hope for and certain of what we do not see."

Another translation, the New American Standard Bible, puts it this way: "Now faith is the assurance of things hoped for, the conviction of things not seen." The King James Version has it this way: "Now faith is the substance of things hoped for, the evidence of things not seen."

All of these translations of the Bible are pointing the same way, yet all are striving to find the richest words possible to describe faith. Faith is the *substance*; it's like the title deed, to what you yet cannot see. When you buy a home, you first walk through a bunch of homes, then you make an offer, and finally you go to a title company to close the deal. After you sign on the dotted line of every page of a two-foot-high stack of papers, you own a home! But you can't see that home yet. You are still at the title company. Who cares — you've got the deed, you've got the *assurance*, you've got the *substance* of it. In a matter of time, you will see it and possess it.

Hebrews 11:2 says, "This is what the ancients were commended for," which refers to the compliments paid to all the people in verses 3 through 29. As you read through these short stories, notice how often the people who acted in faith first received "a word from God," which they obeyed. In other words, their actions were not really their own idea —

rather, they heard something from God, and responded obediently to His call. Faith and obedience are inextricable! God's way often is to give His children a specific instruction and give them time to carry it out. They do not know exactly how they are going to accomplish it or how they will find all the resources they need. Their obedience and adventure that follows become their experience of "walking by faith"

Let's consider some examples from Hebrews 11. Verse 7 says, "By faith Noah, being warned of God of things not seen as yet, moved with fear, prepared an ark" (KJV). Noah didn't just wake up one morning and say, "I want to build myself a boat." No, God gave him a specific command: *Build an ark.* Actually, the ark was not a boat as much as it was a floating box, like a storage chest. It had no sail or rudder. (Where was Noah going to sail to anyway?) The ark was a treasure chest of God containing cherished valuables: the people of faith and the animals of His creation.

Verse 8 tells a similar story. "By faith Abraham, when called to go to a place he would later receive as his inheritance, obeyed and went, even though he did not know where he was going. God said, "Hit the road," and Abraham didn't bother to ask, "Which road?" He just starting walking, believing by faith that God would give him his direction as he needed it.

In this chapter of Hebrews, the same sequence occurs again and again:

1. God gives someone a command; the person hears it as a word coming from God.

2. The person takes action based on what he heard. (He trusts and obeys God's word.)

3. Serious trials confront him, but God sustains him to the completion of his work.

4. Some are victorious (as we see victory); others are defeated (as we see defeat);

but all of them are faithful to the end (as God sees faithfulness) and are rewarded by God.

Every promise that God made to these people was fulfilled. In every story where God promised something, He came through on His promise. One of the things God really wants from His children is to see them live and work and play and struggle, like people who believe that God is who He is and will do what He says He will do. He loves it when you trust Him!

The skeptic says, "Seeing is believing." He taunts faith by crying out, "I will not believe it until I see it." The believer says the opposite: believing *is* seeing. The believer knows, "I will see it only after I believe it." This sounds like a step of blind faith, but it's not that dark. Really, biblical faith (trusting in the promises of God) is a leap into the light! Hearing a promise (or a specific instruction) from God, and then acting on that, *is* the mechanism that brings belief into visible being.

A favorite Bible teacher of mine, the late Manley Beasley, said this: "Act like it is so, when it is not so, in order for it to be so, because it is so." Did you catch that? "Act like it is so (in the spiritual realm), when it is not so (in the visible realm), in order for it to be so (in the physical realm) because it is so (in the spiritual realm). Read that as many times as you need, until you catch it! Your acting "like it is so" is what God is looking for, to "make it so." This principle comes from a passage in Romans 4:17 concerning Abraham's faith, where it refers to God as, "the God who gives life to the dead and calls things that are not as though they were."

Flight of the Phoenix is a great movie depiction of this kind of faith. The original film (1965) starred Jimmy Stewart, while the remake (2004) featured Dennis Quaid. In both films, a twin-engine plane crashes in the desert, and the survivors are in dire straits. They are too far out to walk back, and no one knows their location. One man in the group is a designer of model planes, and he has a vision: rebuild a smaller plane out of the undamaged parts of the wreck. The others struggle to muster up faith in the idea of rebuilding, to say nothing of the idea of actually climbing on board and taking off. It is a great story about calling things that are not as though they were.

In the verses that follow, Romans 4:20–21, we find another compliment to Abraham's faith:

> He [Abraham] did not waver through unbelief regarding the promise of God, but was strengthened in his faith and gave glory to God, being fully persuaded that God had power to do what he had promised.

There's that common theme again: God had the power to do what He had promised. That's the essence of what God wants from you and from me: the recognition by us that He is a God who does what He has promised to do. Walking in faith boils down to this one issue: do you believe that God has the power to do what He has promised to do?

This might be a good time to review those things that God has and has not promised to do. As a primer on God's promises, which of these do you think He has actually promised?

1. That He will never leave us or forsake us (Matthew 28:20). True False

2. That all who live godly lives in Christ will never suffer (2 Timothy 3:12). True False

3. That nothing can separate us from the love of God (Romans 8:38–39). True False

4. That we can understand all the mysteries of life (1 Corinthians 13:12). True False

5. That He will meet all of our needs according to His riches (Philippians 4:19). True False

The true promises are numbers 1, 3, and 5.

Statements 2 and 4 are false.

MY OWN STORY OF FAITH

I was blessed to grow up in a happy home, and my inheritance was the delight of being personally taught to fly by my own father. Believe me, I was carefully taught! I don't think he wanted to send me off flying and then have to tell my mother that I wasn't coming back. He was a good man, and a good father.

He was brought up in one kind of church but had been burned by some bad experiences. My mother also was a person of faith but went to a church that seemed (to us kids) to be harsh and unpleasant. She made us attend Sunday school, but none of us related well to the teaching, nor did we enjoy the people or find any encouragement for daily living. We all dropped out just as soon as we were old enough to stay home alone.

The Boy Scouts provided great training for me in life skills, leadership development, and character quality. So I was "reverent" anytime the subject of God came up, but that did not give me any guidance for finding a purpose in life.

I graduated from the University of Texas, where the school motto is etched on their tall tower: "*You shall know the truth, and the truth shall set you free.*" (John 8:32) I walked past those words every day but never learned that it was Jesus who said them!

Basically, my religion was "American civic patriotism" as expressed by General MacArthur ("Duty, Honor, Country"), and so I became an Air Force officer and pilot and served in Southeast Asia. The Air Force's involvement in the Vietnam War ended just weeks before I arrived, and I found myself as a fighter pilot with no war to fight. We spent months patrolling the borders, trying to believe the line from Milton's poem that "They also serve who only stand and wait."

The long hours of idle time caused me to ponder, *Is this all there is? Flying higher, going faster, and living harder? Surely there is more?* I asked that question of a Christian officer who pointed me to the claims and promises of Jesus. A Bible placed in the base chapel by the Gideons led me to Ephesians 2:8–9 — that passage that says, "For it is by grace you have been saved, through faith — and this not from yourselves, it is the gift of God."

Suddenly, I knew that God's grace was *the answer* for me! In that moment, I knew less about God than you have learned in four chapters. Still, I prayed to God and asked Him to save my soul and "give me a second chance," and something wonderful happened to me that night. I felt a deep peace in the matter and whispered to myself, "Okay, that settles it."

The next morning my first thought was, *I belong to Him*, and my second thought was, *I feel clean inside and out*. When I told my Christian friend what had happened, he invited me to attend a Bible study that he led. Within weeks, I had learned the basic truths that make up the content of this book, and my faith was gaining altitude.

Thirty-five years later, I can attest: every good and beautiful thing that has happened to me since, I can trace back to that night in Southeast Asia, when I transferred my trust to Christ.

The Four Forces of Faith

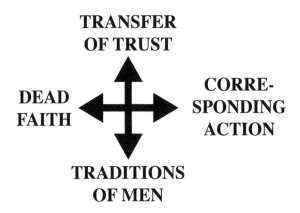

TRANSFER
OF TRUST

DEAD
FAITH

CORRE-
SPONDING
ACTION

TRADITIONS
OF MEN

This chapter has hammered home one truth: that saving faith requires a transfer of trust, from self to God. Faith puts "lift" under your wings and sends you soaring. The phrase "traditions of men" is a biblical expression that refers to those who think they can save themselves by their own good works. They are going nowhere without God. For example, Jesus said, "hypocrites...honor me with their lips, but their hearts are far from me. They worship me in vain; their teachings are...the traditions of men" (Mark 7:6–8).

Many people ask me, if faith is what saves us, then what is the role of "good works"?

One passage that explains the roles of faith and works is found in James 2:14–17—"What good is it, my brothers, if a man claims to have faith but has no deeds? Can such faith save him?" The implied answer would be, "No." That kind of faith won't save anyone. Verse 17 also clarifies this: "Faith by itself, if it is not accompanied by action, is dead." What does the word *dead* do in this sentence? *Dead* is an adjective, which means that it modifies a noun (*faith*). The verse says, in essence, "Any faith that does not produce corresponding action (good works) is dead faith."

Let's sum it up this way: Saving faith will always produce corresponding action. Dead faith, which produces no action, will not save anyone. Here's a short quiz: If someone says that she has faith, but there's no evidence of good works, what does she need?

A) Works, to go along with her faith.

B) Better faith—the kind that saves and produces good works.

If you thought for one second that the answer is A, go directly to the beginning of this chapter and read it again. Hopefully, you nailed B as the solution to the problem of "faith without works."

Chapter Four Quiz

1. Biblical "saving faith" is best defined as:
   a) simply believing that everything will turn out fine in the end
   b) a mental assent (agreement) to the notion that God exists
   c) confidence that I have lived a life that's good enough
   d) totally trusting that God will do what He says He will do

2. On the cross, one of Jesus' final "statements" was:
    a) I've done my part; now it's up to the people to pay for their own sins
    b) I've paid it "in full." The people only need to believe and receive
    c) I've paid the down payment; people can pay the remainder with good works
    d) I've done all I can do; it's in God's hands to decide what He will do later

3. Biblical faith is based on the simple premise that God will do what He says He will do.
    a) True
    b) False

4. In the Old Testament, people were saved by keeping the law. In the New Testament, people are saved by living good lives.
    a) True
    b) False

5. A Bible promise is a statement with two distinct components, which are: (pick two)
    a) prophecy
    b) condition
    c) proverb
    d) benefit

6. In some Bible promises, there is nothing for us to do—the verse simply tells us what God is going to do because of His nature and character.
    a) True
    b) False

7. Once we are saved by our faith (and God's grace), God no longer requires us to exercise faith on a daily basis.
    a) True
    b) False

8. The role of faith and works is best described by which statement:
   a) to be saved from sin, a person needs to have both faith and good works
   b) to be saved, a person needs to have only faith—works are irrelevant
   c) the kind of faith that saves is the kind that produces good works
   d) if a person claims to have faith, it matters not whether they have any works

9. If a person claims to have faith, but no corresponding action (good works) can be seen, what that person needs to develop is:
   a) works to go along with faith
   b) a different kind of faith, that produces works
   c) lots of money, to buy favor with God

10. The chapter in the Bible that is called "The hall of fame of the faithful" is:
   a) Romans 11
   b) Ephesians 1
   c) Hebrews 11
   d) Hebrews 1

Questions for Group Discussion

Get to know others on the flight:

Have you ever been on a flight when things got scary?

Have you had to trust someone else with your life? What was that experience like for you?

Flying higher:

Some people have far greater difficulty trusting than do others. On a scale of 1 to 10, with 1 as great difficulty trusting, and 10 as easily trusting, what number are you?

What circumstances impacted you to make you more or less trusting of people?

Does God, as you know Him prove trustworthy?

Why does it seem easier to trust Christ for our eternal salvation than for rent money?

Is there a faith step God wants you to take in response to this chapter?

Let your imagination take flight:

Picture yourself as one of those people in Hebrew 11. What would you need or want from God to make obedience easier? Do you think you would have obeyed? How would your life have been different had you not obeyed?

Quiz answers: 1d, 2b, 3a, 4b, 5b & d, 6a, 7b, 8c, 9b, 10c

CHAPTER FIVE

A LOVE LETTER, NOT A USER'S MANUAL:
HEAR THE SONG OF THE SKY

Ben and I were happily cruising along in his high-performance single-engine plane. We were approaching our home base in Arlington, Texas, and Ben was piloting the plane. As we circled to line up on the runway for landing, Ben lowered the landing gear handle to bring down the wheels. But nothing happened. Normally we would hear a whirr of an electric motor and an assuring thump as the three wheels locked into place. Not today. No whirr, no thump, no wheels.

We were not in any real danger here, except that we might soon be spending a lot of money on repairs! Pilots have a saying: "Any landing is a good landing if you can walk away from it. And if you can use the plane again, it's a great landing." However, his plane would be grounded for a while if we had to belly-land it while the fire trucks watched anxiously from the side of the runway.

Ben continued to fly while I pulled out a big, thick *Pilot's Operating Handbook*. It's an owner's manual, much like the one you received with your car. Just as you keep yours in your glove compartment, we keep ours right behind the pilot's seat. I looked up the section about landing gear malfunctions, and sure enough, there were instructions for what to do in this situation. After a few anxious minutes, we managed to get the wheels down and then to get ourselves down in a relatively normal landing, thanks to the help of the *Operating Handbook.*

God, in His infinite wisdom, gave us all a *Human's Operating Handbook,* called the Bible. But you don't have to wait until you have some in-life (or in-flight) emergency to reach for this book. The Bible is a great source of daily nourishment, like food or vitamins. In fact, it refers to itself in different places as milk, meat, bread, water, and honey!

The word *Bible* just means "book," and it's really a book of many books, sixty-six in all. One acronym of the word B.I.B.L.E. is "Basic Instructions Before Leaving Earth." For sure, the Bible will give you basic instructions, but please do not approach it as a technical manual. Rather, read it as a collection of stories and sermons and songs. It's the story of God, of His people, of life and death and sin and salvation. In short, it's "the story of God and us."

The Germans found a way to describe the theme of the Bible in a single word. They coined the term *heilsgeschicte,* which translates into English as *salvation history.* What a cool word! It refers to "all the things that God did and God said" in order to bring salvation to us. In other words, the Bible is the history of "His-story." It's the history of God's creative and redemptive efforts to bring to Himself a people who will live eternally with Him for His glory.

The Presbyterians have always understood this well, and in many of their churches, inscribed right over the front doorway to the church, is this visionary statement:

The Chief End of Man Is to Glorify God and Enjoy Him Forever

The Bible is God's written instruction on how to bring that vision to pass!

There are countless other books that speak on these themes, but this one is different. Millions of people over thousands of years have attested that this book particularly seems to have the breath of God upon it. The theological term for having the breath of God on it is *inspired*. In English, inspiration refers to breathing in, as in *in-spiration*. In the Greek language of the Bible, the word for inspired was *theopneustos*, literally *God-breathed*. The Bible has God's breath on it!

The Bible is also said to be *inerrant*, meaning that it does not contain errors. The Bible is not primarily a history book, but when it reports history, it's accurate. You can have confidence in what it says. The Bible is not primarily a science textbook, but when it speaks about science, anatomy, astronomy, or zoology, it's amazingly on target. Critics of the Bible are always looking for errors and often think they have found some. For example, Job 38:16 records God asking this question, "Have you journeyed to the springs of the sea or walked in the recesses of the deep?" For years, skeptics asked, "What springs in the deep ocean?" Then, in recent years, oceanologists discovered that there are in fact springs of fresh water deep in the sea.

Other apparent errors are merely figures of speech, such as "the four corners of the earth" (Isaiah 11:12), which was not intended to state that the earth has corners. Literally, *four corners* represents the four directions on a compass and means from everywhere on the earth.

There are also many paradoxes in the Bible, where it

appears to say one thing in one place and then the opposite in another. At first glance, these statements appear to contradict, but upon deeper study, they do not. Sometimes two witnesses to an event report different details, but that is true of almost all witnesses who report events—different people will have seen different things and, consequently, report different details.

Some of the paradoxes concern things like law and grace, or faith and works, or God's sovereign will versus man's free will. In these cases, the paradox is intentional, as the two elements of one truth actually stand in tension with each other (like a rubber band stretched between your thumbs). Anytime we remove one element we end up with an unbalanced view of the other element. Let go of one side of the rubber band and it snaps the other way. As Yogi Berra might have said, "Life is full of contradictions, and all of them are true."

One more descriptive term for the Bible is *infallible*, meaning that, in matters of morals and ethics, it will not cause you to trip and fall. In other words, the teachings of the Bible work! This is the report of countless Christians who have gone before you, saintly people who have relied upon the Bible for spiritual guidance and found it to be sufficient for whatever life threw their way.

This book is amazingly helpful at figuring out life. It has a truly miraculous ability to communicate to the human soul. It tells of the love that God has for each of His children. Even skeptics who picked it up in order to attack and ridicule it have been caught in its spell. God's Word is a love story about a God who created, lost, loved, and offered to redeem His people. So do not read it as if it were only ancient religious literature. Rather, read it as if it were God's love letter to you — because it's precisely that.

Still, the Bible is ancient. Our English Bible is not only translated from other languages, but from other cultures. The Bible is not easy to understand at first read, but with effort, you can understand enough of it to reap great benefits. The science of aviation is not easy to grasp either, but one does not need to become an aeronautical engineer with a master's in meteorology to become a private pilot. Almost anyone can learn the basics of flying, enough to be able to take off and land a plane. Almost anyone can grasp the major teachings of the Bible, enough for your spiritual life to take wings and fly.

Let's start with the Bible's Table of Contents and break this big thick Bible down into bite-size pieces. The very first step is to see that the Bible consists of two testaments, the Old Testament and the New Testament (think: before Christ and after Christ; or law and grace). The word *testament* basically means "covenant" (an endless partnership), but it also carries the idea of something made in association with a death (say, a last will and testament). The testator in legal language is one who has written and executed a last will and testament that is in effect at the time of his death. Because of the supreme importance of the death of Christ, it's appropriate to refer to the two parts of the Bible as testaments.

With two testaments, it's easy to be confused about which applies today. Is one obsolete? No. Do we need them both? Yes. The New Testament does not replace the Old — rather, it sits on the foundation of the Old, the way a house sits on a concrete slab. The New Testament completes and confirms all that the Old Testament said would happen. The Old is full of types and shadows, of things to come, and the New is full of completions of those things. A clever way to remember that is this: the New is in the Old, concealed; the Old is in the New, revealed.

The Old and the New Testaments each have three sections, and the sections are in a particular order. The Old Testament *historical* books come first. These are narrative books with plots, characters, and conflicts. They read like exciting novels and are generally telling God's story in chronological order. They include Genesis (the beginnings of mankind and of Israel); Exodus (Israel's exit from Egypt and the Ten Commandments); Leviticus (about Levites and priests); Numbers (about offerings and feasts) and many more books.

Then the *writings* section is next. This includes Psalms (which are song lyrics, meant to be accompanied by stringed instruments) and Proverbs (short, self-evident wisdom statements). The prophetic books make up the third and final section of the Old Testament. These were sermons of the prophets. The major prophets, such as Isaiah and Jeremiah, wrote longer books, hence the term *major prophets*. Twelve *minor prophets* wrote shorter books. (God bless them—don't you appreciate a shorter sermon?)

The New Testament is arranged in a similar manner. The *historical* books are the four Gospels (Matthew, Mark, Luke, and John—they read much like biographies of Jesus). These are followed by the Acts of the Apostles, which is an exciting story about the first Christians figuring out how to do church and go on mission (and get persecuted too).

In the New Testament the *writings* are Epistles, which are letters written to a church (or a group of churches) or to a person. In every case, the letters were intended for public distribution. In other words, the apostles were blogging, but since the Internet wouldn't be invented for thousands of years, they wrote on scrolls and had their scribes make copies to be distributed. People read those letters and then made more copies. From the early centuries and through the Dark Ages and Middle Ages, all the way to our age, Christian workers (often Catholic monks) carefully and meticulously made copies and passed them from generation to generation. They used a number of tricks to ensure accuracy, like counting the number of words, and even the number of letters, and even the frequency of occurrence of each letter. Wow! This had to be an incredibly painstaking exercise.

As for prophetic books, there is only one in the New Testament—The Revelation. Although it reads like a book of secrets and mysteries, the title actually means "uncovering." This is a future-oriented book; it gives a series of word pictures about how the end of the age will look. Christians often do not agree on how to interpret the word pictures, so various theories abound as to when and how the end-time events will occur. For now, here's what you need to know: I've read the back of the book, and *we win in the end!* Leave the study of this book until you have become well grounded in the Gospels and Epistles and are walking steadily with the Lord.

Can you see that we have already broken down the whole

Bible into two testaments, and each testament into three sections? You can break it into even smaller bites, by reading and studying one book at a time.

Beyond merely reading the Bible is a whole new adventure of learning to study the Bible. Bible study might sound at first like a dull activity, but believers will tell you that it can be interesting, enlightening—even profitable. Have you ever heard, "Give a man a fish and he will not be hungry today. Teach him how to fish and he will never be hungry again"? That adage applies to Bible-study skills. If you can "feed yourself" from the Word, you will never be spiritually hungry again. In addition, people who really know their way around this book tend to become upwardly mobile—they prosper in business, in social, and in community affairs.

What price would you put on spiritual wisdom? If the Bible helps you grow in spirit and in wisdom and in power for living, bring it on! Learning to study the Bible on your own is not as difficult as you might think. Start by reading a passage and asking several questions that will upgrade your understanding of it.

- Who wrote this?
- Whom were they addressing?
- When and where was this written?
- What is the main subject under discussion here?
- What is the purpose or key point?
- How does this fit in with the passages before and after?

Where is the best place to begin reading in the Old Testament? Some people would say, start with Genesis, the first book of the Bible. Genesis is an exciting story about the beginnings of the world, the human race, and the nation of Israel. But in terms of reading a little bit each day, to take in spiritual vitamins, it's hard to beat Psalms and Proverbs. For example, you could read Psalm 27:1–3 (KJV) the first thing in the morning and quickly see all kinds of strength flowing into your heart and life.

The LORD is my light and my salvation; whom shall I fear?
The LORD is the strength of my life; of whom shall I be afraid?
When the wicked, even mine enemies and my foes,
came upon me to eat up my flesh, they stumbled and fell.
Though a host should encamp against me, my heart shall not fear:
though war should rise against me, in this will I be confident.

Learning Exercise: Psalm 27

1. How does it make you feel to have the Lord as your light and salvation?

2. If you have fearful circumstances in your life, does reading this reduce your fear?

3. Can you read this and then pray, thanking God for this truth in your life today?

As you read the Psalms, it's helpful to know how Hebrew poetry works. English poetry is based on the repetition of sounds. Recall simple poetry like, "Roses are red, violets are blue, sugar is sweet and I love you." The rhyming of blue and you as well as the rhythm of the phrases are what make this poetic. However, in the Hebrew language, it's a repetition of the *ideas*, not the sounds, which make it poetic. For instance, Psalm 1:1 is going to repeat the same thought in three different ways: "Blessed is the man who does not walk in the counsel of the wicked or stand in the way of sinners or sit in the seat of mockers."

Actually, there are two repeating sequences in this Psalm: *walk, stand, sit* makes one. *Wicked, sinners, mockers* makes another one. As you read the Psalms, look for this kind of repetition, or symmetry, everywhere. Read the Psalms as if you were reading poetry, not mathematics. Take in the feel of the Psalm, i.e., the tone, the human emotion, the artistry of it.

It's a good thing that God made Hebrew poetry work this way. Otherwise, we'd all have to learn Hebrew to catch the rhythm of the sounds! Many Bible students do study Hebrew to better understand the Old Testament, and Greek to be able to read the New Testament. It's not that you pick up new information, but the pictures become brighter—something like the difference in watching TV in black-and-white versus color.

If you decide to undertake a study of one of these languages, it would help you to know that Greek is logical and mathematical, while Hebrew is poetic and totally illogical. They have different alphabets but you'll be surprised at how easy it is to learn the shapes and sounds and be able to sound out the text in the original languages. Sounding it out is easy—knowing what it says is much more challenging.

The book of Proverbs is another treasure trove for finding

spiritual nuggets of truth. These brief statements of truth can be as refreshing as splashing cold water in your face first thing in the morning. What makes them unique is how, when you read them, you almost always see the point in an instant—these do not require commentators or ancient-language skills to explain their impact.

To gain godly knowledge is one thing. It implies an acquisition of information and facts about God. To gain wisdom infers an ability to apply that spiritual knowledge to everyday life. Read these four proverbs and see if you don't find instant agreement with the wisdom that is there:

Proverbs 10:5—He who gathers crops in summer is a wise son, but he who sleeps during harvest is a disgraceful son.

Proverbs 17:27-28—A man of knowledge uses words with restraint, and a man of understanding is even-tempered. Even a fool is thought wise if he keeps silent, and discerning if he holds his tongue.

Proverbs 18:12-13—Before his downfall a man's heart is proud, but humility comes before honor. He who answers before listening— that is his folly and his shame.

Proverbs 20:3—It is to a man's honor to avoid strife, but every fool is quick to quarrel.

As to where to start reading in the New Testament, the answer is similar to the Old Testament—you may jump right in at the beginning. The first four books of the New Testament are called Gospels, from an Old English word that meant *good news*. The word picture associated with this term was that of an explorer anchoring his ship in some newly discovered harbor and rowing to shore to claim this land for his king. As his trumpeter sounded the fanfare, the explorer would plant the flag and make a gospel proclamation: "This land now belongs to the king."

Ancient Christians realized that the message of these books is basically, "The human heart that receives this message—this human heart now belongs to the King!" And that's good news.

I remember once flying along in the dark over western Oklahoma, trying to find the small airport just outside of the city of Sayre. I thought it had runway lights, until I arrived there and discovered that the area where the airport should have been was completely dark. I could make out some big hangars along the road to the west, and since the runway ran parallel to that road, I had an idea of where it should be. Landing a plane at night without runway lights is possible, but it's not easy. Our plane had a landing light, like a car headlight, so if we could figure out where the runway was and then maneuver down to a really short final approach (without seeing the runway), then our light would illuminate it just in time for our arrival. The trick was all in the business of lining up with a runway I still couldn't see. I circled over the field and turned where I thought the runway should be, and while about one-half mile out, I caught a glimpse of what would be my salvation. The locals had placed little reflectors down each side of the runway. Those reflectors picked up my landing light, and I could see the whole runway. We slipped on in, and I felt like blowing a trumpet and saying, "Good news—this airport now belongs to me!"

In the Bible, the four "good news" books read like biographies of Jesus. There are four of them, in order to give us multiple pictures of this one man, the God-man who came in the form of a man, to die upon the cross for our sins. They are like four portraits of the same man or four accounts from different witnesses. They each have their own sources, audiences, and points of view, as shown in this chart:

The Four Gospels Seen Together

Four Gospels	Matthew	Mark	Luke	John
presents Jesus as...	King	Servant	Son of Man	Son of God
written for the...	Jews	Romans	Greeks	Everyone
Genealogy to...	Abraham, to show Jesus was Jewish	None: who cares about a servant	Adam, to show Jesus' humanity	see John 1:1
source	Author was an eyewitness.	Author was Peter's aide.	Mary (Jesus' mother) helped.	Author was an Eyewitness.
key verse	5:17	10:45	24:47	20:31
structure	Sermons connected by miracles	Reads like a newspaper	Historical narrative	Series of miracles with stories
themes	Kingdom of God. Old Testament reinterpreted	"Immediately" appears 12 times (a servant word)	women the poor peace/prayer Holy Spirit	The Logos Christ's deity preexistence
location/ date	Antioch late 60s	Rome early 60s	Rome (with Paul) mid 60s	Ephesus late 80s
portion unique to this gospel	59%	7% Almost all of Mark is in Matthew	45%	92% Almost entirely unique

Learning Exercise: The Four Gospels

1) In which gospel would you expect to find the following?
(Use a Bible to confirm the answers)
   a) References to the Ten Commandments
      (check 5:21, 27)
   b) "I am the resurrection and the life." (11:25)
   c) Mary and Martha (at Jesus' feet) (10:38)
   d) The "greatest" commandment (22:36)
   e) "I am the light of the world." (8:12)
   f) The story of the prodigal son (15:11)

2) Which gospel writer is...?
   a) most like a philosopher
   b) more like a reporter
   c) more like a lawyer
   d) more like a counselor

3) Which gospel book would you recommend to a person
who is seeking to know more about the Christian faith, if...?
   a) the person is a Jewish male
   b) the person is a nurse
   c) the person is a journalist
   d) the person is poor
   e) the person doesn't have strong reading skills

Answers:
1: a Matthew; b John; c Luke; d Matthew; e John; f Luke
2: a John; b Mark; c Matthew; d Luke
3: a Matthew; b Luke; c Mark; d Luke; e Mark

Reading a portion of the Bible every day to gain spiritual strength and insight has been the hallmark of dedicated followers of Christ for centuries. A small dose of Scripture first thing in the morning is like a vitamin pill taken with breakfast. And like vitamins, you cannot ignore them for six days, and then gulp down all seven pills on one day and expect to be strengthened for a week.

The secret to success here is to have some plan, some structure, for daily reading. This could be as simple as a bookmark in the Bible or as elaborate as an annual reading plan that identifies a specific passage to read each day for one year. In ten to fifteen minutes a day, it's possible to read the entire Bible in a year.

Bookstores abound with devotional books, which are books that offer a daily reading along with one or more verses. Most of these emphasize what God has done for us, rather than what we are to do for God, hence they are called devotional, or inspirational (as opposed to instructional).

How God Speaks Through the Bible

Of all the explanations in the Bible of how God speaks, Psalm 19 might be the clearest. It describes three ways that God speaks. The first way is through "general revelation," God speaking through nature. Psalm 19:1–3 says:

> The heavens declare the glory of God;
> the skies proclaim the work of his hands.
>
> Day after day they pour forth speech;
> night after night they display knowledge.
>
> There is no speech or language
> where their voice is not heard.

Surely you've been outdoors (or up in a plane) when a gorgeous sunset appeared in the western sky and you froze in your tracks and marveled at it. That the prismatic effect of the sun's rays coming through the dust particles creates this effect is not the point. The point is: *you marveled at it*. The fact that Saturn has rings is nothing but physics. The fact that we drop our jaws in amazement while looking at them, now that is divine!

Back to that sunset—while you were enjoying it, did this thought ever fly through your head: *God made this*? Or as you were looking at tiny flowers, or vast galaxies, or microscopic cells, it suddenly hits you: *God made this*. Study the human eyeball, or the DNA helix. Try to understand how the earth orbits the sun, at just the right distance, with just the right gravity, experiencing just the right seasons and temperatures…and see if God doesn't show up. Likely, this thought will pop into your head at some point: *God made this*.

You can hear from God, or see His handiwork, in any of a hundred different ways and think, *Wow, God did this*. General revelation is where God says, "Hello, I made this," but unfortunately that is about all He says. If I had been God, I might have had the clouds form words like "I love you" or the flowers grow in patterns that spelled out the Word of God. However, God is much more subtle (elegant?) than I. So the psalm shifts gears in verses 7 and 8 (italics mine):

> The *law* of the LORD is perfect, reviving the soul.

> The *statutes* of the LORD are trustworthy, making wise the simple.

The *precepts* of the LORD are right, giving joy to the heart.

The *commands* of the LORD are radiant, giving light to the eyes.

This is talking about God speaking through the printed words in the Bible, and He is speaking much more specifically. Hence, theologians call this *specific revelation*. Note that the emphasized words in verses 7 and 8 sound like literary types that are in the Bible. Most Christians would testify that they hear God speaking through His printed Word more often, and more reliably, than in any other way. Still, in verse 9, the psalm mentions two more channels of God's communication (italics mine):

The *fear* of the LORD is pure, enduring forever.

The *ordinances* of the LORD are sure and altogether righteous.

These communications from God are subjective and elusive. They did not come from black letters on a white page. Perhaps we could call this *personal* revelation. Believers have long known the power of sensing God's presence in every situation. That's what the fear of the Lord means — to be aware that God is here; He's watching and listening. He's very present in the situation. The ordinances could also be translated the "convincings." Another term is *conviction*, which also means *convinced* — i.e., when a jury "convicts" someone, they are *convinced* of that person's guilt.

A SURVEY OF THE OLD TESTAMENT BOOKS

Book	Author	Description (theme)	Key verse/s
Genesis	Moses	Beginnings...Eden to Egypt	1:1; 6:5
Exodus	"	The Way Out (of Egypt & sin)	3:7-8
Leviticus	"	Levites & priests (be ye holy)	20:26
Numbers	"	Offerings & feasts (complaints!)	11:1
Deuteronomy	"	Law a 2nd time (Moses' farewell)	30:19
Joshua	likely Joshua	Conquest of the Promised Land	1:11
Judges	Samuel?	No king ("right in his own eyes")	17:6
Ruth	Samuel?	Faithfulness rewarded	2:12
1 Samuel	Samuel?	Saul anointed king	8:7
2 Samuel	"	David anointed king	7:8-9
1 Kings	unknown	Kingdom divides into Israel & Judah	11:31
2 Kings	"	Descent into captivity	10:32
1 Chronicles	"The chronicler"	Theological interpretation of history	9:1
2 Chronicles	"	A book of revivals (ch. 15, 20, 23, 29, 35)	7:14
Ezra	" (or Ezra)	Ezra calls the people back to the law	7:10
Nehemiah	Nehemiah	Rebuilding the wall around Jerusalem	2:17
Esther	unknown	Esther answers God's call to duty	4:14
Job	Job	Suffering is not always for punishment	23:10
Psalms	mostly David	Israel's national hymnbook	29:10
Proverbs	mostly Solomon	Short and simple statements of truth	3:13
Ecclesiastes	Solomon	Apart from God, life leads to despair	12:13
Song of Sol.	Solomon	A song allegorizing God's love for us	6:3
Isaiah	Isaiah	An overview of judgment and hope	2 Kgs 17:13
Jeremiah	Jeremiah	God does what He said He would do	1:12
Lamentations	Jeremiah	Let us examine our ways, and return	3:40
Ezekiel	Ezekiel	The prophet to the Jewish exiles	3:11
Daniel	Daniel	Fearless obedience leads to blessing	1:8, 9
Hosea	Hosea	God is faithful even when we're not	2:6-7
Joel	Joel	A call to repentance and revival	2:12-13
Amos	Amos	Judgment upon the nations	5:24
Obadiah	Obadiah	A hymn of hate against the Edomites	1:12
Jonah	Jonah	The reluctant missionary	4:2
Micah	Micah	A prophet of the common man	6:8
Nahum	Nahum	Exulting over Nineveh's destruction	1:2
Habakkuk	Habakkuk	A prophet of faith for the future	1:5; 2:14
Zephaniah	Zephaniah	Even Israel will be judged by God	3:13
Haggai	Haggai	The prophet of rebuilding the temple	1:9
Zechariah	Zechariah	A prophet of victory	4:9
Malachi	Malachi	God is sovereign and universal	1:11

A SURVEY OF THE NEW TESTAMENT BOOKS

Book	Author	Description (theme)	Key verse/s
Matthew	Matthew	Jesus as King	5:17
Mark	Mark	Jesus as Servant	10:45
Luke	Luke	Jesus as Son of Man	24:47
John	John	Jesus as Son of God	20:31
Acts	Luke	Expansion of the church	1:8
Romans	Paul	Overview of theology	1:16
1 Corinthians	Paul	Problems in a church	1:10
2 Corinthians	Paul	Divine comfort	1:20
Galatians	Paul	Antilegalism	5:1
Ephesians	Paul	Guidelines for growth	2:10
Philippians	Paul	Joy for Christians	4:4
Colossians	Paul	Christ is Lord of cosmos	1:16
1 Thessalonians	Paul	Remain faithful in life	5:24
2 Thessalonians	Paul	Remain faithful in work	3:12
1 Timothy	Paul	Sound doctrines	3:15
2 Timothy	Paul	Sound conduct	1:13–14
Titus	Paul	Saved for good works	1:15
Philemon	Paul	A slave now a brother	vv. 10–11
Hebrews	Unknown	Christ is better…	4:14
James	James	Proverbs of the New Testament	1:22
1 Peter	Peter	Suffering	4:12
2 Peter	Peter	Growth in virtue	1:10
1 John	John	Assurance	5:13
2 John	John	Perseverance	v. 8
3 John	John	Affirmation	v. 5
Jude	John	Warnings	vv. 3–4
Revelation	John	Prophecy of the end times	1:7

THE FOUR FORCES OF THE BIBLE

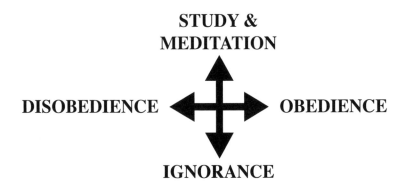

**STUDY &
MEDITATION**

DISOBEDIENCE   **OBEDIENCE**

IGNORANCE

The first chapter of Psalms shows us how the power of God's Word can be like lift under a plane's wings. Psalm 1:3 gives us a word picture of the blessings that come to one who meditates on God's Word. "He is like a tree planted by streams of water, which yields its fruit in season and whose leaf does not wither. Whatever he does prospers."

What kind of meditation are we talking about here? Not Transcendental Meditation, the Eastern practice of emptying one's mind of all thought. Rather, the ancient Hebrews used the term *meditation* to mean the process of filling one's mind with God's Word. To them, meditation meant reading, memorizing, contemplating, singing, writing, talking, and obeying His Word.

In the New Testament, emphasis is not on meditation as much as Bible study, as seen in this example from 2 Timothy 2:15: "Do your best to present yourself to God as one approved, a workman who does not need to be ashamed and who correctly handles the word of truth."

Nothing will thrust your life forward like study combined with obedience. "Do not merely listen to the word, and so deceive yourselves. Do what it says" (James 1:22).

Acting in the opposite direction (rearward), disobedience and ignorance of the Word can do you great harm. The Old Testament prophet Hosea lamented this in Hosea 4:6, "My people are destroyed from lack of knowledge. Because you have rejected knowledge, I also reject you."

Chapter Five Quiz

1. The overall theme of the Bible would be:
   a) all the rules and regulations of religion
   b) all the ways that mankind has failed God
   c) all the words and acts of God to redeem mankind
   d) all of man's ideas and perceptions about God

2. That the Bible is said to be *inspired* means it:
   a) is one of the best-selling books of all time
   b) reads as if it has the breath of God on it
   c) reads so powerfully it takes your breath away
   d) is so brilliant that no human could have written all this

3. The Presbyterians say that the chief end of man is to:
   a) glorify God and enjoy Him forever
   b) glorify God and hope for forgiveness
   c) glorify God and serve Him forever

4. Often what first appear to be errors in the Bible turn out to be:
   a) figments of one's imagination
   b) real errors—after all, no one is perfect
   c) variations in the details of how different witnesses reported the same event

5. The Bible contains many figures of speech that were not intended to be taken literally.
    a) True
    b) False

6. The books about Jesus are called Gospels because:
    a) gospel is another word for God
    b) gospel is a word that means "good news"
    c) gospel is a word that means "biography"

7. There are four gospel accounts of the life of Jesus, because:
    a) Jesus lived four different lives at different times
    b) the Bible intended to give us four pictures of the same person
    c) it took four books to tell everything about Jesus' life
    d) the Bible needed to record every word that Jesus ever spoke

8. The three sections of each Testament include all but which one of these:
    a) prophecy
    b) politics
    c) history
    d) poetry (writings)

9. The term *epistle* means:
    a) a wife of an apostle
    b) a leader of a church
    c) a letter intended for public use
    d) a letter that is a search for truth

10. While the Bible is not a textbook of science or history, where it speaks on these issues, it speaks correctly.
    a) True
    b) False

Questions for Group Discussion

Get to know others on the flight:

Have you ever written a love letter to someone? If so, why did you do it?

Have you ever received a love letter? If so, what was it like to receive it? Do you still have it?

Flying higher:

Are you more apt to read the Bible as an instruction manual or a love letter? For knowledge or for heart change?

Are you comfortable thinking of the Bible as a love letter to you, or are you more comfortable with an instruction manual?

Is Bible study intimidating to you? Why or why not?

Has God ever spoken personally to you through the Bible?

From what you know of the Bible, do you have a favorite book, chapter, or verse? If so, why do you think it is important to you?

What part does the Bible play in *glorifying God and enjoying Him forever*? Is it essential to be reading and studying the Bible to live such a life? Why or why not?

Let your imagination take flight:

Have you ever been hungry? What would it be like to be truly hungry for God and His Word?

For Additional Study: Have you found these quizzes useful? Try out the longer 100-question "Basic Bible Knowledge Tests" found on the author's website: www. whenfaithtakesflight.com

Quiz answers: 1c, 2b, 3a, 4c, 5a, 6b, 7b, 8b, 9c, 10a

Chapter Six

Prayer Is Your Lifeline:

Like Radio Contact with God

In the summer of 1968, a Navy pilot was flying solo in an F8 Crusader jet over central Texas. Suddenly all of the electrical equipment in his single-engine fighter jet shorted out. His radios flickered, and then all died. He could not communicate with anyone on the ground nor could he receive any navigation signals. Although he was cruising in blue sky, beneath his aircraft was a solid layer of thick clouds. They blocked his view of the earth and blinded him from finding his location. He knew the drizzle and rain beneath those clouds went right down to the ground—eliminating any chance of his diving blindly down under the clouds. It looked like he would have to bail out; but first, he made one last desperate radio call on his emergency handheld radio.

"Mayday, Mayday, this is Navy four-two-zero, I am lost and am running low on fuel. My main radios have died. Does anyone hear this transmission?"

Fortunately, the air traffic control facility at Austin heard him and answered his call. The controller on duty that day happened to be my father, Ed Walters, who instructed the pilot to make a left turn and then a right turn. Dad watched all the blips on his radar screen and observed that only one aircraft made those two turns to the left and right.

"Navy four-two-zero, we have you in radar contact thirty miles south of Austin," he said. "What are your intentions?"

There was a brief silence, and then in shaky voice, the Navy pilot answered, "I am open to any reasonable suggestion."

Dad radioed the pilot of a corporate jet that was nearby and asked if he would be willing to help. He agreed, and Dad used his radar to steer the two planes toward a rendezvous. The Navy pilot pulled up "on the wing" of the corporate jet, and Dad then maneuvered them toward the airport at Austin and guided them down through the clouds. The Navy pilot flew his plane right beside the corporate jet, keeping it in sight even in the thick clouds. Once they were popped out under the clouds and lined up with the runway, the Navy plane landed and the corporate jet went on his way.

For Dad, it was another day at the office. For the corporate pilot, it was a chance to help a fellow aviator. For the Navy pilot, it was a close call, and he was surely grateful for the communication channel he had found on that emergency radio.

For the believer living in a relationship with God, who is present but unseen, waiting for an emergency to make contact through prayer is not necessary. You can talk to God anytime, anywhere, about anything. As Christians, we come to God *in Jesus' name.* That expression means that our access to God the Father has been provided by Jesus. It means that through the work of Jesus on the cross, we have a clear channel, so to speak, to approach God. Hebrews 4:14–16 explains this:

> Therefore, since we have a great high priest who has gone
> through the heavens, Jesus the Son of God, let us hold firmly

to the faith we profess. For we do not have a high priest who is unable to sympathize with our weaknesses, but we have one who has been tempted in every way, just as we are—yet was without sin. Let us then approach the throne of grace with confidence, so that we may receive mercy and find grace to help us in our time of need.

So we approach the throne of grace (through prayer) with confidence! What an invitation—come to God the Father in prayer, and come with confidence, seeking mercy and grace. Jesus has made this possible, so we pray in Jesus' name. Often, we say those words in closing our prayer, as kind of a sign-off line, but it's not truly necessary. They are not magic words; rather, they represent our access to God through Jesus' work.

Learning to pray may sound like a tough task, but it doesn't have to be so. Everyone starts out in the school of prayer at a kindergarten level, but as Robert Fulghum famously said, "Everything I needed to know about life I learned in kindergarten." Just get into the habit of making contact with God, and He will develop your prayer power along the way.

Jesus' teaching on prayer centers on a model prayer that He gave His disciples when one of them asked Him, "Lord, teach us to pray." Oddly, there is no record that any of the disciples ever asked Jesus, "Lord, teach us to preach." Yet in our day, there seems to be a lot more preaching than praying going on in church! Let's listen to Jesus' teaching on this vital subject by studying the model prayer, which is often called the Lord's Prayer.

Jesus did not present this as a prayer to be recited word

for word, although we often do it that way in a group setting. Rather, Jesus gave us a model, an outline, for a prayer that covers a wide spectrum of topics. Consider these familiar lines from Matthew 6:9–13 in the King James Version as a simple outline:

The Prayer	The Subject	Explanations
Our Father, which art in heaven, Hallowed [holy] be thy name.	Praise	Commending God for who He is. It is a great way to start any prayer.
Thy kingdom come, Thy will be done in earth, as it is in heaven.	Intercession	Praying for others on a large scale, that God's will may be done in their lives.
Give us this day our daily bread.	Petition, also called supplication	Asking for our own needs to be met.
And forgive us our debts [trespasses or sins] as we forgive our debtors.	Confession	Admitting our shortfalls, thanking God for His forgiveness, and offering it to others as well.
And lead us not into temptation, but deliver us from evil	Guidance and protection.	Appealing for protection. *Deliver* in this sense means "to rescue."
For thine is the kingdom, and the power, and the glory, for ever.	Praise	Praise is a great way to begin and end any prayer. Praise brings you an awareness of God's presence.
Amen.	"Let it be so."	Usually when we say amen, we are saying, "over and out."

You can pray anytime, anywhere, and on any of these topics. It is not necessary to cover all the bases every time you pray. Sometimes your prayer will focus on one urgent need. Other times, you might have a lot to say to God about thanksgiving, or about confession. I've said quick prayers while flying, and long prayers while lying awake at night— it's the attitude, not the word count that matters.

Some believers get confused about whether you need to ask God for forgiveness every single time you sin, or whether it's simply better to thank Him again for His forgiveness of all your sins. Don't worry—either way is fine. The important thing is that you acknowledge two things: 1) your sin, and 2) God's forgiveness. The exact wording or form of your prayer is never important. What's important is your sincerity and humility before God.

Another time-tested outline for simple prayer is found in the acronym A-C-T-S.

A = Adoration (Praise). It's a great way to begin and end any prayer.

C = Confession. Do this before bringing your requests to God.

T = Thanksgiving. It's similar to praise, but more related to what God has done, rather than who God is. We praise God for who He is; we thank God for what He does.

S = Supplication. This is another term for petition (asking).

If there is a secret to prayer, it would be this: prayer in secret. Public prayers and group prayers have their place, but no believer will sustain her flight through life without quiet times of strong, sustaining prayer on her own. Personally, I don't care for long prayers in public. When a preacher prays during a church service, for the first minute, I am praying with him. After about two minutes, I am praying *for* him. If he goes on and on, I find myself eventually praying *against* him!

At its core, prayer is simply having a conversation with God. Ideally, it will be a two-way conversation. That means part of your prayer time needs to be spent listening, and not talking! Silence is an essential part of prayer. If you will read the Scriptures while in an attitude of prayer, you will hear back from God as particular verses suddenly impact you.

Do not expect to hear an audible voice, one that would come to you as sound waves entering your ear and vibrating the little hairs that transmit signals via the nerves up to the brain. No, that's how you hear other people, whose voices are coming to you from across the room. God's voice is going to come to you *from within you,* so it will be more like a still small voice (to use Elijah's words, from 1 Kings 19:12). Isaiah described it this way in Isaiah 30:21: "Whether you turn to the right or to the left, your ears will hear a voice behind you, saying, *'This is the way; walk in it'*" (italics mine).

If your heart is inclined to hear Him, God can speak to you in so many other ways. Perhaps through another person who says something that cuts you to the quick. One line of a song just grabs your heart, and you realize you are hearing from Him! (It could even be one line from a long, dry sermon by your pastor — one line that grabs you by the throat and won't let go.)

Mike Wells, a wonderful teacher of prayer, says, "God will speak to you in a thought-voice that will sound very much like your own voice." This has been my experience over the years — sometimes in prayer a thought will pop into my head, one that I know is not my thought. Where did it come from? Could this be a word from God? How do I know it's not a word from the devil? Doesn't the devil also throw thoughts into our heads? (He can't read our thoughts, but he can throw his thoughts into our heads.) Ephesians 6:16 makes a reference to the "flaming arrows of the evil one," which may be those thoughts that we wish we never had. These are important questions, and here are some helpful answers.

Anytime you believe you have heard from God in prayer, check what you heard against the printed Word of God. God will never speak a word contrary to the Bible. Let's say I was driving home from work, and this thought pops into my head: *I should go and visit a friend who is in the hospital today.* That idea likely did not come from my flesh, as my flesh is tired, and it wants to go home and chill out. Do you think this thought is from God or from the devil? Caring for those who are sick is such a godly activity — this sounds like a prompting from God. On the other hand, if the thought pops into my head, *why don't I stop at the tavern and get drunk instead of going home,* it's clearly not God. His word is very clear on this topic!

Sometimes you have questions on issues where the answers cannot be so black-and-white. Perhaps you've been offered a job, and you are praying as to whether or not to accept the opportunity. Is this God's will for you? You have the thought that you should say yes to this job, but how do you know if this is God's will or just your own desires? How can you discern if an idea is from God or from some other source? First, hold on to it and wait. Perhaps write it down. Then wait upon the Lord to send confirmation by another means, or give you confidence that indeed, this is the direction for you.

Praying about a matter, waiting for direction, and then discovering real peace about it, is a time-tested method of finding God's will. Philippians 4:7 tells us, "The peace of God, which transcends all understanding, will guard your hearts and your minds in Christ Jesus." Think of that inner peace as an umpire, calling your decision "safe" or "out." If there's no peace, take time to re-think the whole question.

Countless Christians have found wisdom in Psalm 37:4, a passage that says, "Delight yourself in the LORD and he will give you the desires of your heart." The idea is, if you are in close communion with God, those desires that are in your heart – they were put there by God.

Pilots are trained to listen carefully to the control tower's instructions. Anytime a pilot is uncertain about what he has heard, he will ask the tower to repeat or confirm the message. On the radio, "five" and "nine" sound a lot alike, but landing on runway five could be a real problem if the tower had instructed you to land on runway nine.

Years ago, an Oklahoma preacher named Edgar Hallock had a wonderful teaching on claiming the promises of God. If he thought he had an idea that was of God, or needed an answer one way or the other, he simply read Scripture and kept reading until one verse grabbed his heart. Hallock believed that God could use any verse in the Bible to speak to any believer on any given day. This is a subjective use of Scripture, of course, and could lead to all kinds of confusion. Still, Hallock's experience (and that of countless believers) was, if you came to God sincerely looking for answers, He would lead you to a verse in His Word that would contain an answer for you.

This is by no means like opening a Bible at random and letting your finger fall to the page with your eyes closed. No one would recommend that kind of random action for finding guidance. Rather, this is simply reading and waiting and listening until some part of God's Word speaks truth into your heart. God *will* give you an answer, but in His time. The Bible itself has countless examples of someone who is struck by a specific word from God in this manner. In Acts 2:16 Peter recognizes that what was happening on that particular day (in the New Testament era) was "what was spoken by the prophet Joel" (in the Old Testament era). Another time Jesus said, "Today this scripture is fulfilled in your hearing" (Luke 4:21). The Bible is more than just a book of morals and principles—it is God's living Word that can speak to any of us on any topic at any time. Hebrews 4:12 says:

> The word of God is living and active. Sharper than any double-edged sword, it penetrates even to dividing soul and spirit, joints and marrow; it judges the thoughts and attitudes of the heart.

Learning Exercise: Write in your own words these descriptive images found in God's Word:

Jeremiah 23:29 —

Romans 1:16 —

Ephesians 6:17 —

Hebrews 4:12 —

When you suddenly "have a word from God" and you try to share with others, very likely they will not be struck at all by the verse you received. This is because God was speaking specifically to you, and not to them! In Romans 10:17, we are told, "faith comes from hearing…the word of Christ." The term for *word* in this verse is not the usual Greek word *logos*, which means "a broad expression or communication." Rather, it is the unusual term *rhema*, which means "a specific utterance." I believe this verse is teaching us that our faith is built up when we have a specific utterance, a particular promise from Christ that comes to us.

You may be asking yourself if God really answers prayers. God always answers prayers, but—He has at least four possible answers to our prayers:

God's first answer is *yes!* You ask for something, and it comes to pass. Jesus said, "Ask and it will be given to you" (Matthew 7:7), and this happens more often than we might think. Our church prints a list of prayer requests that are submitted by the members every Sunday, and we follow through with many of these people. A very large percentage of these requests will receive a "yes" answer. Although I hesitate to call these "routine" prayers, many are prayers like this, where the petitioner is looking for God's support in everyday, routine matters. The vast majority of the time, year after year, I return to my spiral prayer notebook and write "OK" by these requests. My point is, habitually taking routine matters of life to God in prayer will build your confidence and your faith that God does hear and care and answer *yes* to many of your prayers.

God's second answer to prayer is *no!* As in, not happening! Every believer who's ever gone to the Lord with serious prayer requests has experienced this answer. We've prayed for loved ones who were ill, but ultimately they passed away. We've prayed for jobs that we didn't get. We've prayed for relationships that went south. We've undertaken ministry endeavors that fell flat. We've prayed for people who were not believers, hoping that they, too, would open their hearts to God and come to a place of faith, but, alas, it never happened.

Why does God sometimes say *no* to our prayers? Consider these insights from the book of James:

> James 1:6 — When he asks, he must believe and
> not doubt, because he who doubts is like a
> wave of the sea, blown and tossed by the wind.

> James 4:2 — You do not have, because you do
> not ask God.

> James 4:3 — When you ask, you do not receive,
> because you ask with wrong motives, that you
> may spend what you get on your pleasures.

Learning Exercise: Examine Why God Says No to Prayer

Look up the following verses in your Bible and write out the problems revealed:

Psalm 66:18 —

Proverbs 1:28-29 —

Proverbs 21:13 —

Proverbs 28:9 —

Zechariah 7:8-13 —

God's third answer to prayer is *wait!* God's timing is so different from our timing. God is never in a hurry, and He's never late. With God, time is relative. "A day is like a thousand years" (2 Peter 3:8). Albert Einstein explained his own concept of the relativity of time this way: an hour spent with your sweetheart is not nearly as long as an hour spent in a dentist's chair.

Waiting on God is never easy, but it can be a powerful growth experience in your life. The New American Standard Bible translates Isaiah 40:31 this way:

> Those who wait for the LORD will gain new strength;
> they will mount up with wings like eagles,
> they will run and not get tired,
> they will walk and not become weary.

Waiting on the Lord is a great spiritual discipline. Sometimes you wait like a passenger waiting for a plane to land. You sit in the lounge and occasionally look at the sky, hoping the plane will appear. Time goes by, but no plane comes. You are pacing, and craning your neck up into the sky, but it doesn't help. There is nothing you can do but wait, and this kind of waiting teaches you patience.

Other times you wait like a waiter who is at work in a café. (Maybe that's why they are called *waiters*.) You wait on the Lord by serving Him, by tending to His requests. This is active waiting; this is "working while you wait," doing all that you can do, as if it all depended on you, while trusting in God, as if it all depended on God. Both can be true! This kind of waiting teaches you strength.

One of my spiritual mentors, Carlos Gruber, used to say, "When you talk with God, no words are lost; talk on. When you walk with God, no strength is lost; walk on. When you wait upon God, no time is lost; wait on."

God's fourth answer to prayer is *I have something better.* This may be the most difficult answer of all to understand and accept. It feels like a no answer, but as time goes by, and as you wait, things happen, and God leads you in another direction. Sometimes God literally protects us from ourselves and our unwise prayer requests. In Matthew 7:9–11, Jesus explained,

> What man is there among you who, when his son asks for
> a loaf, will give him a stone? Or if he asks for a fish, he will
> not give him a snake, will he? If you then, being evil, know
> how to give good gifts to your children, how much more will
> your Father who is in heaven give what is good to those who
> ask Him! (NASB)

This kind of answer teaches you trust. We can all be grateful that God doesn't always answer our prayers exactly the way we worded them. How fortunate we are that God not only hears our prayers but also sometimes improves them! Romans 8:26 explains that "the Spirit helps us in our weakness. We do not know what we ought to pray for, but the Spirit himself intercedes for us with groans that words cannot express."

Bill Hybels of Willow Creek Church in Chicago has a shorter way of describing God's various answers. In his book *Too Busy Not to Pray*, he uses this clever little outline:

If the request is wrong, God says "No."

If the timing is wrong, God says "Slow."

If you are wrong, God says "Grow."

But if the request is right, the timing is right and you are right, God says "Go!"

Learning Exercise: Spend Extended Time in Prayer

Jesus once asked His disciples to pray with Him on a dark night just before He was arrested. It was late, and they were praying out in a lovely garden. Jesus went a little ways away so He could be alone. When He returned, His friends had fallen asleep! He said to them, "Could you men not keep watch [pray] with me for one hour?" (Matthew 26:40)

Something supernatural happens when you spend an hour in prayer. We love quick prayers, and most of us can say every prayer we know in five minutes. After ten minutes we would be drained and out of ideas. How would we pray a whole hour? What in the world would we do for a whole hour, other than fall asleep, as did Jesus' disciples?

You don't have to ramble endlessly in an hour-long prayer—Jesus said we are not heard for our many words (see Matthew 6:7). Rather, do a number of things that are prayerful in nature: begin with a few minutes of praise and thanksgiving, then stop and read some of God's Word. This will rest your voice and open your heart. Then tell God what you are most thankful for at this time. For a while, just be still and quiet, as if you were sitting in His presence. Confess anything that might hinder your walk with Him. Pray for others' needs. Sing a hymn to God. Read a psalm or any passage where God might speak back to you. Let Him know your own needs—be bold in asking! Finally, return to praising God once more. Let God know that you love Him. This is how you entered prayer; this is how you can exit prayer. End on a joyful and praiseful note!

Voila! If you can spend about five minutes doing each of these activities in prayer, a whole hour will pass. There's no need to set an egg timer; just linger in each activity until you feel prompted to move to the next. What's cool is that it will seem to you more like an hour with your sweetheart than an hour in the dentist's chair. You really can do this, and you will be amazed at the results.

> Much Prayer, Much Power
> Little Prayer, Little Power
> No Prayer, No Power

Are we supposed to kneel when we pray or stand and look up toward the heavens? Why do people mostly tend to sit in a chair, fold their hands, close their eyes, and talk out loud? If I pray while flying a plane, do I have to close my eyes or bend my knees?

Historically, when the Jews of the Bible's day prayed, it was either a) lying face down on the ground, or b) standing and looking up at the heavens. The Bible has other examples of people praying while seated, while walking, while running, while lying down, and while kneeling. Posture doesn't seem to matter. Nor do you have to pray out loud. If someone is pouring out her heart to you, while you are looking into her eyes and hearing her with your ears, you can be praying for her with your heart!

People also lifted their hands up toward God in prayer. Hold up your hands—not as if someone had a gun pointed at you, but rather as if you were lifting up a gift toward God. Arms upward, palms open and up—the gift you are offering to God is your prayer, your heart. All the sections of the Bible have examples of people praying with uplifted hands. Jesus "lifted up his hands and blessed [the people]" (Luke 24:50), and Paul instructed "Men everywhere to lift up holy hands in prayer, without anger or disputing" (1 Timothy 2:8).

Of all the forms of prayer, perhaps the most noble and unselfish prayer is intercession. That word means *standing between* and refers to the prayers one believer makes on behalf of another. It is as if the praying believer *stands between* God and the other person, to make an appeal on his or her behalf. Many times I have taught a person how to fly a plane and then climbed out of the plane to let the student make a first solo flight. As the instructor, I stand beside the runway and watch my student circle the field. I can't do a thing to help—except to pray, and you can be sure all instructors (even the atheists) pray mightily for their solo students!

Intercession is a powerful tool in the hands of every believer. Some Christians are called to serve as intercessors almost as a spiritual calling, a vocation. But even believers who do not have this as a calling should be ready, willing, and able to drop to their knees and lift up the needs of others, even on a moment's notice. Like soldiers, Christians often advance on their knees. Our prayers are powerful weapons that can make the difference in ways that are unexplainable. The Bible is full of stories that exemplify this point.

Jennifer Kennedy Dean, in her book *The Praying Life: Living Beyond Your Limits*, points out a great contrast between what can happen when God's people intercede for one another, as opposed to what happens when they don't. First she tells the story from Exodus 23 where God is angry with the children of Israel who are out in the wilderness and acting unseemly. Just before God releases His wrath to destroy them, Moses intercedes, literally stepping out into the roadway between the people and God, praying for God's mercy and God relents, and spares them.

Dean's second story comes from Ezekiel 22, where the people of God are again in trouble. God decides to destroy them, but His heart is torn, and He says, "I looked for a man…who would stand before me in the gap, but I found none" (v. 30). And those people were destroyed. For the lack of one man to stand in the gap by interceding in prayer, a whole group of people was lost.

Whether the prayer is one of intercession, or of simple petition, Jesus challenges us to do three things in prayer: ask, seek, and knock (see Matthew 7:7). How to remember the order of that verse: His three imperatives spell out the word A-S-K.

Because the verb tenses in the original Greek words for ask, seek, and knock refer to continuous action, not one-time action, a better translation into English would be: "keep on asking... keep on seeking... keep on knocking." Jesus is telling us to be persistent in our prayers; He wants us to be more committed than bringing a simple one-time casual request.

So how long do you keep A-S-K-ing? Here are three signals for you to stop:

#1 When the answer comes. Be sure to say thanks at that point. Jesus once healed ten lepers, and only one came back to thank Him. "Where are the other nine?" He asked the disciples, who shrugged but hopefully got the point. Do we get it? Do our prayers include a ton of Thank You notes?

#2 When you decide you don't really want this to be answered after all. Maybe some time has passed, and upon further reflection, this is no longer something you want to see happen. It is simply no longer your heart's desire. Hey, Lord, thanks for *not* answering that one! As in, "thanks, but no thanks."

#3 When God gives you a promise that it's coming. This is a deeper teaching and relates back to the chapter on faith. Sometimes, when you have some ongoing request in prayer, before you receive any answer, God will send you a promise! Maybe it's something your pastor says or something from the Bible or even a line from a song or a book. Just when you were not expecting it, suddenly there it is—wow! This is a "word from God" for me. God is telling me He *is* going to take care of this.

Once you have His promise, you can stop asking and start thanking Him in advance. This is truly "walking by faith" and will build up your faith as you hear the promise first, stand on that promise (in faith), and finally see the answered prayer before your eyes. Note: this is not "name it and claim it," where you are telling God what you want Him to do for you. No, this is asking, then waiting, then receiving a promise! When the promise comes, then and only then do you have a green light to claim that promise and stop asking for it. So, rather than "name it and claim it," let's call this, "hear it, believe it, and receive it."

One time I was scheduled to go to Nicaragua with a group of preachers on a short-term mission trip. There had been a military uprising the year before, and it appeared that fighting might break out again soon. Our host churches in Nicaragua still wanted us to come, but our home churches and families thought we were crazy. I wasn't sure what to do, but one morning while reading through the Psalms, I came across this passage in Psalm 18: "With your help I can advance against a troop; with my God I can scale a wall" (v. 29). That may not mean anything to you, but in that moment, those words leapt up off the page and said to me: *God is in this thing with us; we can do this mission and do it safely.*

Sure enough, we went to Nicaragua and preached to large crowds every night. One night after preaching, we returned to our little motel to find soldiers waiting to talk to us. For a moment, my heart was in my throat, but they were not there to arrest us. No, they asked me, "Can you tell us how we can know for sure that we will go to heaven if we die in this next war?" And, of course, we could!

THE FOUR FORCES OF PRAYER

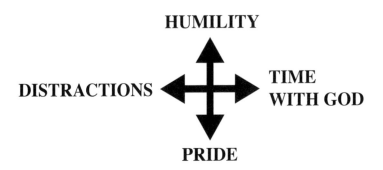

Jesus told the story of two men who went into the temple to pray. One was proud, and one was humble. The proud man stood looking up at heaven, and his prayer went on and on. He had the nerve to say to God, "I am thankful I am not like this other man." Oh, yuck.

Jesus added that the other man was kneeling and looking down at the floor. That man's brief prayer was like a text message: "God be merciful to me a sinner." Only seven words, yet Jesus tells us that the humble man (and not the proud man) was the one who reached God. Pride will weigh down your prayers and keep them from flying up toward God.

Jesus told another story (see Luke 10:39–42) about two women who were hosting Him in their home. One was busy in the kitchen, while the other was seated at Jesus' feet and giving all of her attention to Him. The busy one fussed at Jesus, in effect saying, "Lord, make my sister come and help me get dinner ready." However, Jesus was concerned with things other than dinner. Here's how He answered her: "You are worried and upset about many things, but only one thing is needed," and that one thing was time with Jesus in prayer and devotion. Time with Jesus pulls you forward—do not let distractions hold you back.

Chapter Six Quiz

1. The longer the prayer, the better.   True False

2. It is permissible to express any emotion to God in prayer. True False

3. The Bible teaches us to sit and close our eyes when we pray. True   False

4. God already knows what we need and want, so there is no need to ask. True   False

5. It is not okay to "call down fire" on our enemies; we are to bless them in prayer. True   False

6. What are God's four answers to prayer: _____, _____, _____, _____.

7. What does the memory jogger A-C-T-S mean? _____, _____, _____, _____.
(hint: they are synonyms of praise, apology, gratitude, petition)

8. Praying for others (intercession) may be the noblest form of prayer. True False

9. Humility is an indispensible attitude for successful praying. True False

10. Prayer works better if you are down on your knees.
True False

Questions for Group Discussion

Get to know others on the flight:
We build relationships through talking and listening. Are you more apt to talk or to listen? Does this also apply to your relationship with God?

Do you believe in miracles? Have you ever experienced an answer to prayer that seemed to be on the miracle level?

Flying higher:
Which of these are obstacles for you to developing a strong prayer life?

Believing that He is listening

Believing that He cares

Time and schedule issues

Pride — I can do it on my own.

Which is strongest: a daily prayer time, or an ongoing conversation with God throughout the day?

When have you experienced these answers to prayer?

yes_____

no _____

wait_____

What is the most important prayer request you have at this time?

Let your imagination take flight:

How do you think Jesus is responding to your prayer need right now? Can you envision His face? His posture toward you? His eyes?

Quiz answers: 1 False, 2 True, 3 False, 4 False, 5 True, 6 Yes, No, Wait, Something Better; 7 Adoration, Confession, Thanksgiving, Supplication, 8 True, 9 True, 10 False

CHAPTER SEVEN

MAKE CHURCH WORK FOR YOU:

FLYING IN FORMATION IS FUN

Have you ever been out by a lake when a big flock of Canadian geese appears overhead? First, you hear all the honking, and when you look up, there is the lovely V formation of geese. They circle the landing area and then glide down to the ground. Have you ever wondered why they fly in that V formation? Because it's too hard to form a Z formation! No, the real reason is by staying close to one another, they can fly in the draft of the bird ahead of them, so that the force of drag is reduced. This allows all the geese behind the leader to save a little energy—and yes, they do take turns flying the lead position. In addition, flying in this formation makes it simple to keep track of all the geese in the flock.

Fighter pilots have been using formations like that since airplanes were invented. In the Vietnam era, fighter pilots rarely went into combat without the mutual support of other aircraft. In aerial combat, there is safety in numbers. My instructor explained that enemy pilots had a special term they would use to describe any of our pilots who were separated from our formation. The term was, "Easy Pickings!"

Geese and fighter pilots are not the only ones who thrive by flying in formation. All Christian believers fare better when they are connected to other believers. Following Christ can be dangerous business. Dark forces in the spiritual realm love to spot a Christian who is cut off from mutual support, and what those forces then think is: here are some easy pickings.

Still, people often ask me, "Hey, pastor, is it possible to be a Christian without having to go to church?" Sure, it's possible, but why would you want to? You can jump out of a plane without a parachute, too, but why would you want to?

You can be a football player without a team, too, but you'll have to throw it, then run really fast and catch it yourself. Just think, after you set the ball on a tee and kick off, you can run clear down the field, grab your own kick, and return it for a touchdown—because there will be no one to tackle you. But what fun is that?

Learning to walk with Jesus is not an individual sport. It is a team activity, and the best place to find your place on the team is in a local church. A good Sunday service is like a spiritual filling station—your tank may be low when you arrive, but the experience should refuel you for the week ahead. Church is not a building, by the way. The term *church* refers to the "called out assembly of people." We are called out by God, to be His people, to gather and worship Him, to hear His Word, and find His will. Church is something *you do*, not someplace you gather. Instead of saying, "We're going to church," we should say, "we are going to do church." Church is a way of life more than a place.

In the Old Testament, the local assembly of Israelites

was called the *synagogue* (another word for "assembly"). The Israelites had one temple, in Jerusalem, but they had a synagogue in every village where they could round up at least ten righteous men. Why the number ten? Likely they remembered the story of Abraham interceding for the city of Sodom. Abraham pled with God to save the city, and God told him that if there even ten righteous men there, He would spare the whole city. The Jews concluded (correctly) that even a small number of people, who meet together and minister together, can bring God's favor upon an entire city!

Jesus Himself attended synagogue services regularly, and then one day He said, "On this rock I will build my church" (Matthew 16:18). The rock Jesus was referring to was Himself, as He is called the *cornerstone* of the church (see 1 Peter 2:6). The first generation of Jesus' followers formed what we call the *early* church. Not early as in 6:00 a.m. in the morning, rather, early in the church era that began with Christ. As I write this, the year is A.D. 2009 (for Latin *Anno Domini*, year of our Lord).

These first followers of Christ were mostly Jews. To separate themselves from regular Jews, the Christian Jews began to meet on Sunday, the first day of the week. They used that day because it was on a Sunday that Christ's empty tomb was found. He had risen from the dead, in accordance with the Bible's prophecies. Christ first appeared to His followers, next He appeared to crowds of people, and then He ascended into heaven, right in front of their eyes. Shortly afterward, the believers in Jerusalem met for their annual remembrance of the feast of Pentecost, at which time they were electrified by an outpouring of the Holy Spirit on their meeting. In the Old Testament, the Holy Spirit (that part of God who is everywhere) came *upon* people temporarily. Now, since the work of Christ was completed, the Holy Spirit began to *permanently indwell* people.

A whole new era, the church age, was underway with the birth of the church. Followers of Jesus Christ were quickly identified as "Christians" shortly after His death and resurrection. The term *Christian* meant "little Christ." The followers themselves referred to their new spiritual movement as "The Way," and the writers of the New Testament Epistles used the term *church* to refer mostly to local congregations (but also to the church universal, the body of believers everywhere).

The early Christians weren't very well organized, and in fact they suffered persecution from the Roman Empire for three full centuries before Christianity was recognized as a legitimate religion for citizens of that day. Once the empire recognized the churches, they soon became a part of it, as the Roman Catholic Church was organized across the Mediterranean world. *Catholic* means "universal," and the Roman Catholic Church continues to be the largest network of churches in the world.

Protestant is the term applied to most non-Catholic Christian churches. The term came from the Middle Ages (1100–1500) when people like Martin Luther and John Calvin led "protests" against Rome for alleged corruptions within church doctrine and practice. Luther's motto was "Only by Grace, Only by Faith, Only the Scriptures." He longed for a simpler, purer church. Churches that have since sprung from the Protestant Reformation include Lutheran, Presbyterian,

Baptist, Episcopal, and others.

Traditional Protestant churches conduct a service that centers on a liturgy, which is a predetermined order of service. Their pastors know in advance which Bible verses to read, what songs to sing, and the topic of the teaching. There are advantages to this kind of service—it is predictable, familiar, and covers all the topics in the Bible over a long season. The design is meant to enhance your opportunity to mentally and spiritual move through the service into worship and contemplation.

Another style of church service that is popular in America is contemporary worship. On any given Sunday, contemporary churches may sing any spiritual song or teach from any book in the Bible. The service may be a bit more spontaneous and may seem more like a celebration than a church service. These churches will say, "God is alive and well, and we are here to praise Him and celebrate His goodness to us."

Regardless of style, the purpose of church is to help believers fulfill the purposes God has put into our lives. Rick Warren's popular book *The Purpose-Driven Life* spelled out five activities for believers' lives: worship, fellowship, discipleship, ministry, mission. Being a part of a local church can help you accomplish all of those things. A strong church exists to reach people with the gospel message, teach them the Christian life, win their hearts for Jesus, and develop them as disciples.

Churches have all kinds of strategies for accomplishing this. Pastor Reg Cox of the Lakewood Church of Christ uses a three-point approach: preaching for inspiration; classes for information; home groups for transformation. That church "exists to be a community of people who are dedicated to loving God and loving others by imitating Christ with a Spirit-filled passion."

Willow Creek Church in Chicago pioneered a kind of church that is driven by a passion to "turn irreligious people into wholly devoted followers of Christ." Wow, that sounds like a challenge—taking agnostics and developing them into missionaries! Yet Willow Creek is now one of the largest and most influential churches in the world. They are a demonstration of the power of the local church. Their pastor, Bill Hybels, likes to say, "The local church is the hope of the world."

Certainly, the local church is where the spiritual growth action is, and beyond all the training and serving, it has another function. Church is where Christians gather to make a home away from home, to become like a small town in the big city, to create something very special and wonderful, something we call *community*.

Although the vast majority of people in America will say they are Christians, only about a third of Americans are active in any local church. Why is that? One might be tempted to think that the reasons might be:

- People are too busy in other activities.
- People are too tired on weekends.
- People don't really take their faith seriously.

Actually, research shows those are not the main reasons. Here's what people say:

#1 Church is boring and repetitive (same old thing every Sunday).

#2 The preaching is irrelevant (not addressing current challenges in life).

#3 They don't relate to church music (or the child-care program is substandard).

#4 Churches place too much emphasis on giving money.

Curiously, none of those reasons are theological—they are not about religious beliefs. Rather, they are sociological—they relate to the packaging of the message rather than to the message itself. If the last church you attended had those issues, there's a simple answer: *Find Another Church!*

What did you do that time when you were at the airport, hoping to fly somewhere, and your flight was grounded because of a mechanical problem or just cancelled for whatever reason. You found another flight—that's what you did and that's how you got where you were going. So, if your last church let you down, get back up and try church again, somewhere else.

Truthfully, there are also deeper reasons that people drop out of church. Did something unfortunate happen a long time ago? Perhaps you were offended by a preacher, or some people in church treated you poorly. Or there was a conflict, and you didn't care for the outcome. Or, in a worst-case scenario, you were verbally, emotionally, or physically abused by someone in the church.

Sadly, those things happen, because all churches operate within that broken, fallen world. What happened to you was bad, your pain was real, and I wish it could have been avoided. Nevertheless, you do have some options in how to deal with this, and some are better than just remaining bitter. Bitterness, by the way, will not serve you very well. Holding on to bitterness against church is like drinking a dose of poison hoping a bunch of other people get sick. Why not consider this: what happened to you was unfortunate, but it is now God's problem to deal with. Can you pray through what happened and give the problem to God? Then the next best thing for you to do is find a new church home that will help you grow.

Learning Exercise: Which of these sound like valid purposes for a church? Which would help you live the spiritual life you want, and the life that God would want for you? My own answers are after the list of questions.

1. A country club for saints (placing them in the "in" group with God) True False

2. A haven for sinners (a place to come for redemption and healing) True False

3. A house of prayer (prayer by the people, and for the people) True False

4. A place to be seen by others (making one appear to be religious) True False

5. A small town in the middle of a huge city (an extended family) True False

6. A safe house for Christians (a place to hide from the world) True False

7. A school for servants (a place to learn how to serve others for God) True False

8. A launching pad for missionary enterprises (local and global outreaches) True False

My answers: # 2, 3, 5, 7, and 8 are valid purposes for a church.
#1, 4, and 6 are not.

Every believer needs to find a local church that works. At first glance, that might not sound difficult, once you decide to find it, but in reality, searching out and finding one's home church may be as complex as finding and buying one's own home. Here are some guidelines to help you in your search:

Poor Reasons to Select a Church

1. It is located closest to your house.

2. It has a denominational name with which you're familiar. (That name doesn't tell you much anymore, except how the church is governed. Every denomination has a wide spectrum of churches operating with different styles, purposes, and programs.)

3. Someone recommended it to you (but didn't actually take you there).

4. The building (or the pastor) is attractive.

5. The people were friendly (or helped you pay your rent).

Good Reasons to Select a Church

1. You attended a service and left feeling spiritually refreshed.

2. The Bible was taught and explained in a way that was beneficial to you.

3. Their beliefs are consistent with what you believe to be true about God and life.

4. At the service, you heard, sensed, or felt God's presence.

5. Every time you go, you are inspired to make a difference in the world around you.

6. You have an indefinable sense that you belong there; this is the place for you.

When I was a new believer and the Air Force transferred me to Lubbock, Texas, I had no idea where to go to church, yet I was desperate to belong in church somewhere. I visited several, but the experience was like trying on shoes in a shoe store. Just a few steps and I knew these were not the shoes (or the churches) for me. Finally, I received an invitation to a midweek church supper and, being a single man at the time, couldn't refuse. I showed up on time, but the fellow who invited me forgot to come! There I was on the front porch of a church, watching people nod a silent greeting to me as they went inside. After some time, one man, Charles McCown, took time to converse with me and learn of my dilemma. "Come inside and sit with us," he offered, which are magic words to any first-time visitor at a church. Over dinner, he found out what I did for a living (teaching flying) and introduced me to another pilot. I made a new friend quickly, and that man introduced me to the pastor. By the end of the evening, I was pretty sure I had found my new home, in terms of a local church.

How to Succeed at the Church You Select

1. Show up. Keep showing up. It takes awhile to become comfortable in any church.

2. Find a worship service that works for you, and sit in the same area each week. Be friendly and get acquainted with the people around you. Take the initiative here.

3. If the church has adult classes or groups, take the plunge! This will be a little scary, but you absolutely will not make friends at a large church if you only attend the worship service. Smaller classes and groups are where the action is — if one doesn't work for you, try another one. You will be so encouraged when at last you find your place.

4. Attend any lunches, fellowship gatherings, picnics, etc. This is where you'll find out if the church is open to new people or closed into cliques who have been there forever.

5. Participate in a service project where volunteers are requested. This is absolutely the best way to plug in, feel the

pulse of the church, and discover for yourself that this is your place to call home.

    6.   Contribute to the church financially. Jesus said, "Where your treasure is, there your heart will be also" (Matthew 6:21).

The Two Ordinances of the Church

Twice, Jesus made it a point to conduct a special religious practice and instructed His followers to continue with the practice (and there is evidence that they did continue with it). Since He ordained these rituals, we call them ordinances. There are two: baptism and the Lord's Supper.

Baptism in water is offered to people by different means. On the occasion of the birth of their child, parents will have the child baptized into their church. This is *infant baptism*, almost always accomplished by sprinkling water on the baby's head. Some churches believe this ceremony has real impact on the salvation of the child's soul. Other churches practice this more as a form of family dedication.

Believer's baptism is offered on the occasion of one's conversion, that is, one's personal acceptance of Christ into one's life as Lord and Savior. This usually occurs when the person is at least six years old (when he or she is able to understand abstract concepts), and this baptism may be done by sprinkling or by immersion. Baptists are strongly identified with immersion, but many other churches practice this mode of baptism. Usually the person performing the baptism goes down into the water with the baptismal candidate and gently lowers the person into the water (and quickly raises him back up).

In two places in the New Testament (Acts 8 and Acts 16) we find a kind of formula for how a person comes to Christ and is baptized:

1. A person hears the story of Jesus and His death on the cross.

2. That person believes the story and repents of his sin, putting his trust in Christ.

3. The person gives a verbal confession that he has placed his trust in Christ.

4. He is then baptized... and goes on his way "rejoicing" or "with great joy."

It seems that believer's baptism represents the final step in a series of actions that propel a person forward in spiritual progress.

The second ordinance is called either Communion, or the Lord's Supper (depending on which church is conducting it). This rite is not a meal, but rather the eating and drinking of a very small amount of bread and wine. Usually the bread is unleavened (made without yeast, so it is flat, like a cracker). Often the wine is mere grape juice, out of consideration to the temperance virtue and also to those who have had substance-abuse problems with alcohol. The basic symbolism of these elements is clear: the bread leads us to remember the body of Christ, broken for us; the wine or grape juice leads us to remember the blood of Christ, poured out for us. The exact theological understanding of why we use these elements is a matter of wide debate.

Catholics teach the idea of *transubstantiation*, meaning that a miracle takes place. While the outer essences of the bread and wine or juice remain the same, in a spiritual sense they actually become the body and blood of Christ. This is based on a literal rendering of Jesus' statement in Matthew 26:26–28.

> While they were eating, Jesus took bread, gave thanks and broke it, and gave it to his disciples, saying, "Take and eat; this is my body." Then he took the cup, gave thanks and offered it to them, saying, "Drink from it, all of you. This is my blood of the covenant, which is poured out for many for the forgiveness of sins."

When Jesus said, "This is my body," most Protestants believe He was using a metaphor. Therefore, Lutherans and Reformed churches hold to a concept of *consubstantiation*, meaning they believe the essence of God is *present along with* the bread and wine or juice. Still other churches, like Baptists, hold to the idea that the entire ceremony is *symbolic*. The purpose of the ritual is to remind us of Jesus' body and blood, so there is no need for the elements to somehow transform themselves into those very things.

Whichever church you join, and however they do their service, church is the place where you can form strong bonds of friendship with fellow church members. When you pray together, sing together, eat together, work together, and at times go through struggles together, you become like "foxhole buddies." Have you ever noticed how soldiers who fought together in the same unit remain friends for life? Military pilots would spend hours and hours in the briefing room, then more hours on boring patrol. Suddenly a battle would break out, and their hours of boredom were punctuated by moments of sheer terror. The survivors would invariably keep in touch and be friends for life.

Hopefully your church experience will not involve terror! Still, you can form friendships that will serve you all the days of your life.

THE FOUR FORCES OF CHURCH

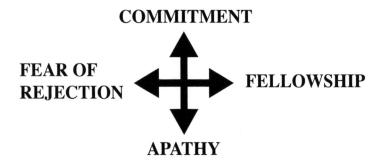

COMMITMENT

FEAR OF
REJECTION   FELLOWSHIP

APATHY

The power of commitment is readily seen when a person or family gets involved in a church. When you give the best you have in service to others, the best quickly comes back to you. People who thrive in a local church have a sense of John F. Kennedy's famous challenge: "Ask not what your [church] can do for you, but what you can do for your [church]."

In the New Testament, the early Christians met together often, both on the first day of the week and, at times, every day of the week. Since they did not have church buildings yet, they met in homes or in all kinds of public places, both indoors and outdoors. In Acts chapter 2, Christians are said to be meeting together for prayer and worship, eating together in their homes, praying together, and serving together. But apparently, apathy has also been a problem since the early church. In Hebrews 10:25, believers were cautioned, "not give up meeting together, as some are in the habit of doing, but let us encourage one another — and all the more as you see the Day approaching."

Chapter Seven Quiz

1. Most usages of the term *church* in the New Testament refer to the local church, not the universal (worldwide) church.
   a) True
   b) False

2. In ancient Israel, there were many temples but only one synagogue.
   a) True
   b) False

3. The early Christians began to meet on Sunday in order to:
   a) avoid the persecution of the Romans
   b) save Saturday for a day of recreation
   c) separate themselves from the other Jews

4. The resurrected Christ appeared to:
   a) his female followers
   b) his male followers
   c) a whole crowd of people
   d) all of the above

5. Which of the following is not a good use of a local church building?
   a) creating a place to come and pray with others
   b) developing a safe haven for Christians to avoid other people
   c) gathering people for worship and teaching on Sundays
   d) training children to be strong believers in Christ

6. One good use of a church building is to create a sense of community within a city.
   a) True
   b) False

7. According to the Bible, there is one specifically correct way to do church services.
   a) True
   b) False

8. Participating in a service project is a good way to connect as a new church attender.
   a) True
   b) False

9. Attending and participating in a small group or class is optional for success at church.
   a) True
   b) False

10. Which of these is not an ordinance of the church, according to Jesus?
    a) baptism
    b) covered-dish supper
    c) Communion (Lord's Supper)

Questions for Group Discussion

Get to know others on the flight:

Did you grow up attending church? If so, what are your memories?

If not, what was your first experience of attending church like?

What was your funniest church experience? Your saddest?

Flying higher:

If you currently attend a church on a regular basis, why do you do so? If not, why not?

Have you ever been baptized? What was the experience like for you?

What do you believe you can contribute (or do now contribute) to the church community?

Let your imagination take flight:

If Jesus moved into your community and began to look for a church, what would He look for?

If you were going to start a new church in an area where none existed, what would it be like? Describe your idea of a church service.

Describe the outreach you would do to attract new people. Does your church do some of these things now?

Quiz answers: 1a, 2b, 3c, 4d, 5b, 6a, 7b, 8a, 9b, 10b

CHAPTER EIGHT

IS MONEY YOUR SERVANT
OR YOUR MASTER?
KNOW WHO'S IN COMMAND

An Air Force student pilot was piloting our T-38 jet from the front cockpit while I observed from the instructor's seat in the back cockpit. He pulled the plane up into a big loop, and we felt our bodies pressed down into our seats, as the positive G forces built up due to centrifugal force. Then he rolled the plane upside down, and we would have fallen out of our seats were we not tightly strapped in by our shoulder harnesses. Putting the plane in this negative G mode is very uncomfortable. While I hung there upside down, flecks of dust and dirt floated around the cockpit. We were making loops and rolls in the sky, first climbing high and then diving fast. Next, he slowed the plane down to where it was barely hanging in the air, to show me he could fly it at minimum controllable airspeed.

For just a moment, he let the plane get too slow, and the wings stalled. Instantly the plane rolled hard to the right, and we were upside down. There was no need to panic, as we had plenty of altitude to recover, but panic he did! He jammed the throttles forward from idle power to full afterburner power, a bad idea when the plane is going so slow. The air flow over the compressors in the two engines became disrupted, so both engines quit in the most audibly spectacular manner I have ever witnessed. In other words, it suddenly got real quiet! The normal roar of the jet engines was replaced by a strange silence. We were like one of those sailplanes you sometimes see floating gently through the sky, except that a twelve-thousand-pound jet trainer glides more like a boat anchor — straight down!

For the last half hour, the student had been flying the plane. Now he had lost control — and the plane was flying him! Because he no longer had any real control of the plane, he was in reality only a passenger. Unless we could start at least one of the engines, we would have to eject from the crippled plane and float down in our parachutes. Most likely we would live to tell about it, but if you leave an Air Force base in one of their jets and then return to base on foot, carrying a parachute over your shoulder, they do ask a lot of hard questions.

This particular jet airplane doesn't come equipped with starters for its engines. On the ground, we started them by using a machine to blow air through the turbines, causing them to spin up to speed. In the air, you can restart an engine only one way: by diving toward the ground. This works pretty well if you have enough altitude and at least one engine is willing to come back to life, and quickly. I took control of the plane and shoved it into a dive, while doing some quick math in my head. From 18,000 feet, diving at 6,000 feet per minute, we had two minutes before reaching the minimum safe bailout altitude. Either we would regain control, or we would have no choice but to pull the ejection handles that would blow the canopy off and launch ourselves out of a very expensive falling jet plane.

Our speed zoomed up, the student pressed the ignition buttons, and fortunately, both engines spun back to life. Whew! We flew back to base without further incident. The lesson was learned: if the student loses control of the machine, the machine will take control of the student. This is true of airplanes; it is also true of Christians and their money.

Money management is the acid test of the Christian life. It separates those who follow Jesus with all their hearts from those who follow Jesus more as a hobby. Jesus threw down the gauntlet when He spoke these words in Luke 16:13:

> No servant can serve two masters. Either he will hate the one and love the other, or he will be devoted to the one and despise the other. You cannot serve both God and Money.

In other words, every follower of Jesus needs to tame the money monster. Either you serve God and let your money serve you, or you end up serving your money instead of God. The truth is: money is either a great servant or a terrible master.

Why do we have to have money anyway? Doesn't the Bible say money is the root of all evil? Actually, no. The Bible says, "*The love of money* is a root of all kinds of evil" (1 Timothy 6:10). The love of money has driven people to do all sorts of unwise things. The money itself is neither good nor evil. How we use it, how we manage it—that's what makes it good or evil.

The biblical term for money management is *stewardship*.

Being a steward just means being a manager. To be a steward, you manage money or resources for another.

Suppose you walk into a small store and ask this question of a clerk: "Sir, are you the owner of this store?" The clerk might say, "Well, I am the manager of the store, how can I help you?" Instantly you know that this person is not the owner. He told you he was the manager (the steward), and so you know right away he is not the actual owner.

The issue for you is this: *who owns your store (your money, your possessions)?* In Psalm 50:9–12, the Bible makes it clear that God is rightfully the owner of everything.

> I have no need of a bull from your stall
> or of goats from your pens,
> for every animal of the forest is mine,
> and the cattle on a thousand hills.
> I know every bird in the mountains,
> and the creatures of the field are mine.
> If I were hungry I would not tell you,
> for the world is mine, and all that is in it.

If God is the owner of everything, and if He has assigned you to be the manager (steward) of some stuff, your perspective changes. Your motto becomes, *this money is God's money; I am just managing it for Him.* This car trouble is God's car trouble; I will look to Him to provide for the repairs. This bill I cannot pay is really God's bill; I will trust Him to show me how to pay it. Perspective is powerful. With this viewpoint, money becomes less stressful.

The Old Testament taught the Israelites to give 10 percent of their income to God. This would include income from their jobs, their crops, or their vineyards. They gave God the first 10 percent, and they lived off the other 90 percent with His blessings. The classic verse on this is Malachi 3:8–10:

> "Will a man rob God? Yet you rob me.
>
> "But you ask, 'How do we rob you?'
>
> "In tithes and offerings. You are under a curse—the whole nation of you—because you are robbing me. Bring the whole tithe into the storehouse, that there may be food in my house. Test me in this," says the LORD Almighty, "and see if I will not throw open the floodgates of heaven and pour out so much blessing that you will not have room enough for it."

This is one of the few places in the Bible where God says, "Test me in this." He literally dares us to give Him a chance to show that He is a keeper of promises. His ability to give to us far exceeds our ability to give to Him. Countless Christians, who make the tithe to God the basis of their financial security plan, will testify that God can be trusted with finances. Give Him 10 percent, and He takes the other 90 percent, stretches it, adds to it, and multiplies it for you.

According to Malachi, your only other option is to act like a thief and rob Him of the tithe. The famous preacher R. G. Lee once preached on this Malachi passage and opened his sermon by greeting his congregation this way: "Ladies, Gentleman, and Thieves." God's commitment to bless the tithers is a Bible promise—and don't let anyone tell you that is only for Old Testament believers. No sir—the Bible says in 2 Corinthians 1:20 that all of the promises of God are valid "in Christ." That is, they are available to all believers, Old and New Testament.

Jesus comes along in the New Testament and does not teach tithing in the Old Testament way. Rather, He makes it tougher; in Luke 14:33, He says, "Any of you who does not give up everything he has cannot be my disciple." Jesus is not demanding total poverty of His followers; rather, He is asking for total control, for ultimate ownership, of His followers' material possessions.

Jesus did affirm some men for tithing (giving 10 percent), but He put it in perspective when He added, "But you have neglected the more important matters of the law—justice, mercy and faithfulness" (Matthew 23:23). Jesus was saying that while giving money was good, it is no substitute for showing justice and mercy to others.

One day, a young man came to Jesus with a question. We don't know his name, but he ends up being called "the rich young man." He wanted to know how to get to heaven, and Jesus' first answer to him was, "You know the commandments." The young man claimed to have obeyed them all of his life, but he still had no peace in the matter. Jesus looked at him, with a heart of love, and then said to him, "Go, sell everything you have and give to the poor, and you will have treasure in heaven. Then come, follow me" (Mark 10:21). Wow, that's a tough demand, at least for this young man, for the Bible says he could not rise to that challenge and went away sad. You may own a car, a home, or an airplane and have worked your whole life to obtain it. The true test remains: do you look at it and say, "This is mine"?

The command to give it all to the poor is not a universal

command to all believers, so don't panic. But why did Jesus give it to this one man? Perhaps it was because the man trusted in his riches far more than he trusted in God. This cowardly young man could not grasp that following Christ means serving Him instead of serving money. Had the man accepted the challenge and walked away from his riches, he would have quickly found that trusting Christ brings more satisfaction than trusting money. Over time, he might well have been blessed financially in return, as it is God's nature to respond generously to those who have proven themselves capable of handling money properly.

Pat Robertson, the founder of the Christian Broadcasting Network, was so moved by this story that as a young Christian, he did give away all of his wealth and possessions (to the shock and horror of his wife, who was out of town at the time.) His autobiography, *Shout It From the Housetops*, goes on to tell how God showed Pat and his wife how to live on little income. Then God showed them how much greater were the blessings of faith, once they regarded money as their servant rather than their master. Years later, God entrusted Pat Robertson with millions and millions of dollars, which were used to create the first Christian television network in the United States.

Randy Alcorn, author of *The Treasure Principle*, had a similar experience. Circumstances led him to voluntarily downsize his lifestyle to that of a minimum wage, while at the same time he was able to give away virtually all of the royalties from books he had written. As his books became more and more popular, he and his wife were able to give away incredible sums of money, far beyond anything they had ever imagined. Still living a simple lifestyle, they testify that they enjoy life now more than ever.

What about ordinary Christians, all of those who haven't written books or started television networks? We do not think of ourselves as rich, but the truth is, compared to the vast majority of the people alive on earth today, we are all rich. Yes! If you live in a comfortable home, have plenty of food in the kitchen and, most likely, a car or two in the garage, you are rich! So what instructions does the Bible give to those who are rich? It might surprise you to learn these instructions, found in 1 Timothy 6:17–19:

> Command those who are rich in this present world not to be arrogant nor to put their hope in wealth, which is so uncertain, but to put their hope in God, who richly provides us with everything for our enjoyment. Command them to do good, to be rich in good deeds, and to be generous and willing to share. In this way they will lay up treasure for themselves as a firm foundation for the coming age, so that they may take hold of the life that is truly life.

Let's take these one by one. First, those of us who are rich should not become arrogant. That's not asking too much, is it? Second, let us not put our hope in wealth. Who would argue with that wisdom? Third, we are to put our hope in God. Fourth, we are to "do good, to be rich in good deeds." Gee, so far we have heard four instructions and we haven't yet reached for our wallets. Finally, number five does say, "Be generous and willing to share." We can do that. In fact, wouldn't you agree that *all five of these instructions* are both reasonable and doable?

When we handle money properly, God does bless us. But what does that blessing look like? Is it always financial? Would we say that if we give generously, as per the instructions, God will necessarily and always return financial blessings to us? Honestly, I would not say that. Many other variables might determine how God would bless us. Here's what you can count on, according to the famous Bible teacher Dwight Moody. Moody said, "The blessing of the Old Testament era was prosperity. The blessing of the New Testament era was adversity." And may I add, "The blessing for all time (and our time) is contentment."

The sign of God's blessing in your life today is seen neither in riches nor in poverty. Rather, it is seen in this: that you have contentment, in whatever circumstance you find yourself. This is a huge key to keeping one's spiritual life from crashing when tough times come and financial crashes occur.

Another source of wisdom on money management from God's Word is the book of Proverbs. Consider these gems of short, self-evident wisdom:

Honor the LORD with your wealth, with the first fruits of all your crops. (Proverbs 3:9)

He who is kind to the poor lends to the LORD, and he will reward him for what he has done. (Proverbs 19:17)

He who loves pleasure will become poor; whoever loves wine and oil will never be rich. (Proverbs 21:17)

The rich rules over the poor, and the borrower is servant to the lender. (Proverbs 22:7)

For most Americans, the difficult issue in finances is not a lack of income but rather an excess of expenses. Easily available debt, through the constant barrage of credit-card offers, has created huge misery for countless people. Several Christian ministries are now dedicated to helping believers eliminate their debts and find financial freedom (another way of saying, financial contentment). Crown Financial Ministries (www.crown.org) offers classes and materials for every life situation. Author and speaker Dave Ramsey (www.daveramsey.com) is widely recognized as an expert in helping believers eliminate debt.

A few years ago, I came close to buying an airplane that a friend was selling. (What pilot is there who hasn't dreamed of owning his own plane?) The purchase price wasn't too high, and the interest rates were low. But when I began to add up all the costs of fuel, maintenance, insurance, storage, and taxes, honestly counting the cost of this undertaking, the real price of the project was way beyond my means. Wisdom prevailed, and I found a way to fly by joining a time-share club where thirty pilots share two planes. This costs me only a fraction of what it would have cost me had I bought a whole plane. It's humble, but it's also much less stressful.

The bottom line of money management: almost anyone can improve his financial situation by taking three key steps that will be recommended in almost any Christian financial-planning tool.

Number one: resolve to operate as one of God's stewards, not an independent owner. Make a commitment to begin giving to God, either through your local church or directly to godly causes of missions and ministries to the poor. Some believers will jump into the deep end of the pool and just start tithing (and countless numbers of us will tell you that it works). Others will tiptoe in, giving a small amount at first and increasing it incrementally until the 10 percent goal is reached. Something supernatural happens to your finances when you are giving 10 percent—this is hard to believe, but you can "test God" on this and see it for yourself.

Number two: make a budget for your household. It can be so complex that you have it on a computer or so simple you can use a big yellow tablet; either way will work. The trick is to have a plan of how much you will spend on lifestyle and debt reduction, and each month monitor how you are doing compared to your plan. If your outgo exceeds your income, your upkeep will be your downfall.

Dieters know that keeping a food journal is a powerful tool for losing weight. Keeping a money journal, a record of expenses, will have a similar effect. Once you really see where your money is going, you will soon be keeping better watch over it. Planning is everything in financial management. To fail to plan is to plan to fail!

Number three: attack the debt. Stop piling it up, and start trimming it down. Cut up credit cards if necessary. You can start paying off the highest interest accounts first, or you can use the snowball method: pay off the smallest account first, while making minimum payments on the others. Once the smallest one is gone, add that payment amount to the minimum on the second account. This will eliminate the second smallest account soon, and you can add what you were paying on accounts one and two to number three. This snowball grows larger and larger as you pay off the smaller accounts, and finally you are attacking the largest, and last, account.

Learning Exercise: See if you can match these non biblical proverbs with their authors.

1. When money speaks, the truth keeps silent.	a) Ben Franklin
2. In God we trust, all others must pay cash.	b) Yiddish proverb
3. To know what a man is really like, take notice of how he acts when he loses money.	c) Russian proverb
4. A penny saved is a penny earned.	d) Sen. Everett Dirksen
5. A billion here, a billion there, and pretty soon you are talking about real money.	e) American proverb
6. With money in your pocket, you are wise and you are handsome and you sing well, too.	f) Simone Weil

Answers: 1c, 2e, 3f, 4a, 5d, 6b.

THE FOUR FORCES OF MONEY

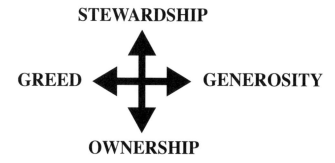

STEWARDSHIP

GREED ◄————► **GENEROSITY**

OWNERSHIP

"No one can serve two masters. Either he will hate the one and love the other, or he will be devoted to the one and despise the other. You cannot serve both God and Money." When Jesus said this, in Matthew 6:24, He laid down the primary principle of money management. If we think we own our money (or our stuff), we are serving it. Once we believe God owns our money, we become stewards of God, and the money serves us. Stewardship, then, is a lifting force. Ownership, acting to the contrary, weighs us down.

"Be on your guard against all kinds of greed; a man's life does not consist in the abundance of his possessions" (Luke 12:15). This is another quote from Jesus, who talked more on the topic of money than on any other single topic. Jesus warned against greed because it is the greatest threat to financial contentment. If you can apprehend this truth and make it your own, you will enjoy the triumph of generosity over greed. Greed will steal the wind from beneath the wings of your spiritual life-- whereas generosity will carry you upward like an eagle soaring on the mountain breezes.

Chapter Eight Quiz

1. Money is the root of all evil.
   a) True
   b) False

2. If a believer gives 10 percent to God, the other 90 percent is theirs to control.
   a) True
   b) False

3. The root issue of stewardship is:
   a) God wants you to be poor
   b) God Himself is poor
   c) God wants you to give it all away
   d) God wants you to be His money manager

4. The New Testament does teach and affirm the practice of tithing.
   a) True
   b) False

5. The rich young man's true spiritual issue was:
   a) peer pressure
   b) trust in God
   c) tradition
   d) lifestyle

6. Jesus talked more about money than about any other topic.
   a) True
   b) False

7. One Bible book that emphasizes money issues is
    a) Psalms
    b) Proverbs
    c) Philippians
    d) Philemon

8. God's blessing in Old Testament times was often indicated by:
    a) adversity
    b) prosperity
    c) contentment
    d) liberty

9. According to D.L. Moody, God's blessing in New Testament times was often indicated by:
    a) adversity
    b) prosperity
    c) contentment
    d) liberty

10. God's blessing in all time (including our time) is indicated by:
    a) adversity
    b) prosperity
    c) contentment
    d) liberty

Questions for Group Discussion

Get to know others on the flight:
In what stage of your life were you most content? Why do you think this was so?

In what stage of your life were you most discontent? What contributed to that feeling?

Flying higher:

Describe what someone who loves money might be like.

Everyone struggles to some extent with greed. How significant is it for you?

How have you experienced God's blessing as a result of your giving?

Have you been in situations where you had to rely on God for your daily needs?

How did He provide?

Are you afraid of giving generously? If so, what are you afraid of?

How much faith would it take to commit to giving 10 percent of your income for six months?

Let your imagination take flight:

You have just been given $1 million, but you can't keep any of it for yourself. How and where would you give it?

Quiz answers: 1b, 2b, 3d, 4a, 5b, 6a, 7b, 8b, 9a, 10c

CHAPTER NINE

DISCIPLES ARE LIFELONG LEARNERS:

ALWAYS GAINING ALTITUDE

When student pilots first arrive at a flying school, they are given a medical exam. Upon successful completion of the exam, each student receives a small piece of paper called a *Medical Certificate and Student Pilot Certificate*. It says the student has passed a physical and enrolled in school, but that's all. It makes no claim about the student's ability to fly. What gives students the ability to fly is their active involvement in the learning experience.

In the same way, joining a church (or being baptized) may provide someone with a piece of paper (church membership), but it makes no claim about one's being a true disciple, a learner and follower of Jesus Christ. The proof of that comes from a person's personal walk, his or her involvement in the spiritual learning experience.

When I was a new pilot, my flight instructor pounded this truth into me: "The day that you stop learning about flying is the day you will become an accident looking for a place to happen!" This is true for followers of Christ also—we must be lifelong learners—lifelong students of the things of God. Or we can become complacent backsliders looking for a place to crash and burn. When you hear the word *disciple*, you think of it as a religious word, right? The term usually refers to someone who is a religious follower of some person, i.e., a "disciple of Christ" or perhaps in a darker usage, a "disciple of some cult leader."

It might surprise you to learn that the term *disciple* actually means "learner" rather than religious follower. The word got into the English language from the Latin root *docere*, meaning, "To learn"; in fact, we have a whole gang of English words coming from this root:

disciple = the person learning

discipline = the process of learning

doctrine = the information you are learning

doctor = the person who has learned

I don't know about you, but when I go see a doctor, I sure hope he is a "learned" doctor! I hope he is a medical *disciple* who applied himself diligently to the *doctrine* with *discipline*. That way, he continues to increase in skill and wisdom, so as to perform with ever-increasing success. It's vital that you see yourself first and foremost as a *learner* about Christ, rather than just someone who *believes* in Christ.

Church membership is a good thing, but merely joining a church does not turn a person into a Christian, any more than joining the Moose Lodge would turn you into a moose! Becoming a true follower of Christ is not about making a one-time commitment or taking any superficial vows. What makes you a disciple of Christ is having His Spirit in your heart, His blood covering your sins, and His place as Lord in your life. That means receiving Christ as Savior, and it also means following Him as Lord. Lord means "master," one who must be obeyed. Once a person has received the benefit of having Christ as Savior, there is also the obligation to follow Him as Lord.

People ask, "Can a person receive Jesus as Savior and *not* receive Him as Lord?" That's a tricky question, because a lot of people receive Christ first as their Savior, without having yet learned what it means for Him to be Lord. Therefore, the best answer to this question is, *Yes, a person can come to Christ and receive Him as Savior only. However, no person can receive Christ as Savior and then later reject Him as Lord.*

The issue is not *when* people learn that Jesus is Lord as well as Savior. Rather, what's essential is that once they learn, they respond. The calling is to make Jesus Christ Lord of your life, to give Him control of the direction of the rest of your life. He leads, we follow.

Part of what that means is being a lifelong spiritual learner. As your entire Christian journey becomes a learning adventure, you soar to new destinations of faith and discover whole new levels of spiritual living.

How long a person lives becomes less important than how a person lives. In fact, a person might wonder, if heaven is ready and waiting, and grace has redeemed me fully, *why wouldn't God just bring me home now?* This leads to the great question of purpose — why in the world is anyone here? Why are you, for example, taking up space on a crowded planet? The answer is twofold.

First, God wants you to have time to mature spiritually.

God wants to grow you and mold you so that over a long period of time, you more and more take on the character qualities of Christ who is "the image of God" (2 Corinthians 4:4). In this way, when you do finally arrive in heaven and meet Jesus face-to-face, it won't be like meeting a total stranger.

Second, God has work for you to do. He wants to use your gifts, talents, and skills like tools in His hand, to make a difference in the lives of the people around you. You do not have to be a world leader to do this. Mother Teresa once said, "We do not do great things for God. We only do little things for a great God." Nor do you have to have great ability. It is your *availability*, more than your *ability*, which God is after. Once you are available, there are actions you can take to keep on growing toward spiritual maturity.

So, what does spiritual maturity look like? At our church, we came up with a Portrait of a World-Moving Christian, a set of seven characteristics and lifestyles that are common to Christians who make a difference for God and His kingdom. Some of these people travel across the world; others might only go across the street. But all of them make a difference wherever they serve.

Portrait of a World-Moving Christian

1. Walks with God in a grace-based relationship through strong personal faith.

2. Knows the basic teachings of the Bible; finds daily nourishment from its words.

3. Enjoys a prayer life that is more than perfunctory; stays in close touch with God.

4. Stays connected to other believers through church, Bible study, and mentoring.

5. Practices good stewardship as one who is a manager of possessions, not the owner.

6. Uses his or her spiritual gifts, talents, and passions to make a difference.

7. Loves God and others as the number one priority in life.

Do these sound familiar? They are the topics we have been discussing in the previous chapters!

John the Baptist was a man who understood well the significance of growing in Christ. He may be the only Bible character who had a "personal mission statement," which is found in John 3:30: "He must become greater; I must become less." Less of me and more of Jesus in me— there's a mission statement that will propel you forward.

As your spiritual knowledge increases over time, your understanding of God will also need to grow. The more you know about what God is like, and about how God has revealed Himself to mankind, the more spiritually mature you will be. To be in any intimate relationship, you need to know what the other person is like, what he prefers and what he dislikes, what brings him joy and what brings him pain. This is true of your relationship with God as well.

After Jesus' spiritual experiences on earth, He explained to His "learners" (the apostles), that He was going to be with the Father. He said this to them: "All this I have spoken while still with you. But the Counselor, the Holy Spirit, whom the Father will send in my name, will teach you all things and will remind you of everything I have said to you" (John 14:25–26).

In that one verse, you can see the entire Trinity (God the Father, God the Son, God the Holy Spirit). The term *Trinity* is a word that Christians use to refer to God existing as Three Persons. Although the word *Trinity* does not appear in the Bible, the concept is in many verses, such as the one above (John 14:25), or in Matthew 28:19, where Jesus says, "Therefore go and make disciples of all nations, baptizing them in the name of the Father and of the Son and of the Holy Spirit."

This passage from John 14 is Jesus' introduction to the Holy Spirit. He also gives the Holy Spirit the title *Counselor*, using a word that could also be translated "comforter." Jesus tells the disciples in verse 16 that the Father is sending the Holy Spirit, and Jesus uses words that mean "another comforter exactly like me," who is "called alongside you to help you."

The Holy Spirit is truly "the Spirit of Jesus." Much of our Christian growth comes from this helping and teaching ministry of the Holy Spirit. These titles for the Holy Spirit are intended to let us know that this Holy Spirit is "exactly the same kind of helper" to us, that Jesus was to the apostles. Just as Jesus was closely present with the apostles — teaching, counseling, comforting — so, too, the Holy Spirit is closely present with you and me.

Consider these three actions that the Holy Spirit takes in our lives: baptizing, filling, and gifting.

First, we are said to be "baptized" into the Holy Spirit by Christ. The term *baptize* means "to immerse." For example, one immerses a bucket into a well to fill it with water. It is a flexible metaphor that is used several ways in the New Testament. One application is the Christian observation of "water baptism," which will be explained in the next chapter. Here I am referring to "spiritual immersion." It is the job of the Holy Spirit to immerse you into Christ the second you receive His grace into your innermost being.

Second, we are said to be "filled" with the Holy Spirit. This language is intended to represent continual action — we are "being filled" over and over with God's Holy Spirit. Why do we need continual refilling? The answer is: because we leak! We fight the daily battle with three enemies: the world, the flesh, and the devil. This "unholy trinity" wants to seduce us to make two mistakes that the Bible notes as unfortunate.

The first mistake is called "grieving" the Holy Spirit (see Ephesians 4:30). This is disappointing God in the manner of, say, a maiden rejecting the wooing of a man who is courting her. It happens when we don't listen to God or don't act upon His promptings. Also, if we fail to give proper time and dedication to our relationship with Him, it causes our relationship with God to be less intimate.

The second mistake is "quenching" the Holy Spirit (see 1 Thessalonians 5:19, NASB). The New International Version says it like this: "Do not put out the Spirit's fire," as in stifling or choking off the power of God within us. This happens when we flat-out disobey His Word or allow ourselves to be ensnared in some sinful behavior. God just will not allow His blessings to flow into us, through us, if we have quenched His Spirit.

Both of these actions are harmful, but neither one can cause us to be separated from God. No, because we are also said to be "sealed in the Holy Spirit." Many verses in the Bible testify to the fact that once we are "in Christ," there's no getting out of that state This is because we are not "hanging on to God" with our faith; no, God is "hanging on to us" by His power! Even if we become faithless, he remains faithful (see 2 Timothy 2:13).

Third, we are said to have received "gifts" from the Holy Spirit. The topic of spiritual gifts has been a source of much confusion, so let's clarify what these mean. The "giftings" (small gifts, or small graces) of the Holy Spirit are not merit badges given to a few deserving folks who are superspiritual. Nor are they magic wands by which one can do parlor tricks and amaze the crowds. When you see "spiritual gift," think of a tool. Think of a believer who has been equipped to perform a spiritual ministry. For example, the gift of mercy is God's equipping of some believers to be especially adept at listening to and consoling people who are in hard times. The gift of teaching is usually accompanied by a passion for studying, preparing, and presenting truth. Gifts like these are called *motivational* gifts and are found listed in Romans 12:6–8.

Another list in 1 Corinthians 12:4–11 describes *miraculous* gifts like faith, healing, and tongues (the ability to speak in an unlearned language or even a totally unknown language, in prayer). These have generated controversy over the years, and a full discussion of them would require more space than can be allotted within this book. Suffice it to say this: don't worry about any gifts you don't have. Rather, determine what gifts you do have and put them to good use! The following exercise may be helpful in figuring out which gifts are operating in your life today.

Learning Exercise: Suppose you came upon an automobile accident just after it happened. Cars are wrecked, some people are injured, and others are frightened. What helpful actions would you naturally be inclined to take (assume that you suddenly had the courage to take these actions)? Circle the ones from this list that would apply to you, and then consult the answers below.

1. Pray for all the people who are involved or affected by the accident.

2. Provide a blanket and comforting words to those who are frightened.

3. Call the police, and organize the traffic flowing around the wrecked cars.

4. Explain to witnesses what you saw and how the accident occurred.

5. Offer to give a ride to anyone who is stranded.

6. Pray for the injured people to be healed by God from their wounds.

7. Give appropriate assurance to people who are upset by the accident.

Answers (spiritual gifts associated with these helpful actions)

1. Intercession (praying for those in trouble)

2. Mercy (listening, consoling, and calming troubled people)

3. Leadership (taking initiative, organizing, delegating, administering)

4. Teaching (telling the truth about what you know for sure)

5. Helping (assisting, serving)

6. Healing (interceding and bringing healing to bear)

7. Encouraging (giving appropriate positive reinforcement, bringing hope)

Another way to determine your spiritual gifting is to simply experiment by doing a number of different service and study projects to see which ones were both successful and rewarding. For example, popular teacher Beth Moore had no idea she had a teaching gift until she became immersed in the Bible through a ladies' study that she subsequently was asked to teach. Her students responded eagerly and brought new people. She discovered she loved the challenges of preparing and speaking, and her giftedness was soon evident to all.

Conversely, a man at our church learned that his gifts did not include teaching, after he began a weekly study that quickly dwindled to no one but him. On the third week, he arrived and found no one but himself in attendance. As he sat quietly pondering this, a maintenance man passed down the hall, and not seeing the one person seated within, turned out the lights! My friend said, "I took that as a sign to find other avenues of ministry and service."

So be bold and experiment with different ways of serving people. Remember, God can equip you with various gifts as you journey through the seasons of life. He wants to use your life experiences, wisdom, personality, and interests, to love and to help the people around you. As you serve others, you cannot help but grow yourself—and that means your faith is flying high!

THE FOUR FORCES OF SPIRITUAL FORMATION

SPIRITUAL APPETITE

HEART DISTRACTED BY THE WORLD

HEART OPEN TO GOD

SPIRITUAL COMPLACENCY

Jesus said, "Blessed are those who hunger and thirst for righteousness, for they will be filled." (Matthew 5:6). An appetite for righteousness will bring you satisfaction, according to Jesus. This holy ambition will be the wind beneath your wings, to take you to a higher walk with God!

On the contrary, spiritual complacency will keep you down in the doldrums. Jesus had this to say to lackadaisical believers, "I know your deeds, that you are neither cold nor hot. I wish you were either one or the other! So, because you are lukewarm—neither hot nor cold—I am about to spit you out of my mouth" (Revelation 3:15–16).

Matthew 13:3–8 presents Jesus' parable about a sower of seed, who scattered his precious seed in different places. Some fell where the birds stole it. Other seed fell on rocky ground and failed to thrive. Still other seed ended up among thorns and was choked. Only the seed that fell into the good soil produced a crop many times over what was sown.

Jesus then explained the parable to his disciples, in verses 19–23:

> When anyone hears the message about the kingdom and does not understand it, the evil one comes and snatches away what was sown in his heart. This is the seed sown along the path. The one who received the seed that fell on rocky places is the man who hears the word and at once receives it with joy. But since he has no root, he lasts only a short time. When trouble or persecution comes because of the word, he quickly falls away. The one who received the seed that fell among the thorns is the man who hears the word, but the worries of this life and the deceitfulness of wealth choke it, making it unfruitful. But the one who received the seed that fell on good soil is the man who hears the word and understands it. He produces a crop, yielding a hundred, sixty or thirty times what was sown.

The point of the parable is: let your heart become good soil!

Chapter Nine Quiz

1. The root meaning of the term *disciple* is:
   a) church member
   b) Christian
   c) learner
   d) follower

2. Which one of these is *not* a reason for God to leave a believer on earth for years and years?
- a) to grow that person toward Christlikeness
- b) to give that person time to make up for his or her mistakes
- c) to use that person as an instrument to influence others for Christ

3. Which of these is not a basic component of the believer's spiritual-growth process?
- a) walking with God in a grace-based relationship
- b) developing a consistent prayer life
- c) wearing Christian clothing and jewelry
- d) connecting to other believers through Bible study and mentoring

4. The term *Trinity*, used by Christians to describe God, does not appear in the Bible.
- a) True
- b) False

5. Which person (part) of God is everywhere all the time?
- a) God the Father
- b) God the Son
- c) God the Holy Spirit

6. Believers can address their prayers to God the Father, to Jesus, or to the Holy Spirit.
- a) True
- b) False

7. Which of these terms is not a description of the Holy Spirit?
- a) Counselor
- b) Comforter
- c) Controller

8. The gifts of the Holy Spirit are like merit badges given for good behavior.
   a) True
   b) False

9. One way to figure out your spiritual gifts is to experiment with different ministry activities.
   a) True
   b) False

10. Serving others (doing ministry) is an activity that will cause you to grow spiritually.
   a) True
   b) False

Questions for Group Discussion

Get to know others on the flight:

Did you enjoy school? Why or why not?

What are some ways that you enjoy learning?

Flying higher:

How would you rate yourself on the Portrait of a World-Moving Christian points?

What (or who) has helped you the most on your own journey as a believer?

Whom are you helping now to grow in faith?

What is your own "holy ambition"? Is your heart open to the things of God?

What are the hindrances in your life to learning more about God and His Word?

Let your imagination take flight:
What do you want your character and countenance to be like when you are eighty years old?

What do you want to be most knowledgeable about during your senior years?

How do you want to be described by those who have known you best?

Quiz answers: 1c, 2b, 3c, 4a, 5c, 6a, 7c, 8b, 9a, 10a

CHAPTER TEN

ALL OF HIS COMMANDMENTS
BOILED DOWN TO ONE:
HOW HIGH WILL YOU FLY?

It had not been one of my better flights. The weather was bumpy most of the way, and I let the plane drift off course twice. Then I made a radio call on the wrong frequency, which was embarrassing. I missed my ETA (estimated time of arrival) by a full ten minutes, and when we finally arrived, I was *so* ready to be back on the ground.

After lowering the plane's wheels and flaps, I glided it gently over the runway and then flared for the landing. The plane floated a few seconds and then the tires kissed the runway and we were rolling out to a stop. Yes—a totally lucky landing. It was a "grease job" landing, as in when someone has greased the runway so you can land smoothly. My passengers were so pleased with that landing. As they happily deplaned, one of them commented that I was surely the greatest pilot since Lindberg. Boy, how little did he know about my flying skills that day! Landings really do have that effect, whether in a plane, or on a spiritual journey.

When you nail the landing, it seems to cover a multitude of other faults. As we bring this book in for a landing, let's turn our attention to one more vital lesson. If you master this one, it can cover "a multitude of faults" in your spiritual life.

One day a man asked Jesus, "Which is the greatest commandment?" (Matthew 22:36). I can imagine him thinking, *Jesus, there are just far too many commandments in this Old Testament. Can you boil it all down to just one?* Jesus gave him a clear answer, with a direct quote from Deuteronomy 6:5. This verse was so well known to Jewish men that they had a title for it — the Shema — meaning, "to hear." (Picture a Navy captain speaking to his crew through a bullhorn: "Now hear this!")

So Captain Jesus says, "'Love the Lord your God with all your heart and with all your soul and with all your mind.' This is the first and greatest commandment" (Matthew 22:37; also Deuteronomy 6:5). Jesus continued, "And the second is like it: 'Love your neighbor as yourself.'" Aha. Another quote from the Old Testament, this one from Leviticus 19:18.

So the man asked for one, and Jesus gave him two. As your flight instructor, I count *three* elements to this "greatest commandment."

First, love God.

Second, love your neighbor.

Third, love yourself (you need this in order to love your neighbor).

Put it all together and you get this: Love God, love your neighbor, and love yourself, with all your heart, soul, and mind, and your spiritual flight through life will be successful.

According to Jesus, love is the number one commandment, out of hundreds of commandments. Live a life characterized by loving, and you are living the way God intended you to live!

Wow, love sounds like a lot more fun than religion. Aren't you glad Jesus didn't say,

"The greatest commandment is… (circle any of these options you would prefer over love):

a) Pray for an hour a day on your knees.

b) Give everything away and live in poverty.

c) Master perfect discipline in every area of life.

d) Attend church every single Sunday, or else.

e) Be miserable and weep and mourn all the time.

Do you realize that Jesus selected a commandment that virtually everyone can keep! You do not need a deep intellect, or a great education; you do not need physical fitness, health, wealth, or political power to do this. Anyone can love God and his neighbor and himself.

The challenge is to do it with all of your heart, soul, and mind. In my experience, I have encountered just a few people who were able to love fully and wildly. These were children who were afflicted with Down's syndrome. Children with that particular developmental disability stay very childlike even while they grow into physical adulthood. They lack certain adult traits like guile, pride, shame, fear, lust, and selfishness. In their own innocent way, they truly love God, their families, their friends, and even people they just meet—

with all of their hearts, souls, and minds.

Ernest Thompson Seton, in his book *The Gospel of the Red Man*, said that many Native American tribes would hold kids with Down's syndrome in very high esteem. They believed that those children were *divine*. Without a scientific pathology to explain these kids' nature, the Native Americans simply observed their incredible love and figured that God put these kids here to show the rest of us what He was like. What an amazing observation that was! The Down's kids may actually be here to show us what God is really like!

Learning Exercise: So, what does it mean for us to love God "with all your heart and all your soul and all your mind"? Circle the action words (verbs) in these verses that instruct us how to love God on every level:

1. We can worship with our *hearts* (our innermost consciousness, our "spirits").

Proverbs 3:5 — Trust in the Lord with all your heart and lean not on your own understanding.

Jeremiah 29:13 — You will seek me and find me when you seek me with all your heart.

2. We can relate with our souls (our emotions, will, and devotions)

Psalm 4:4 — In your anger do not sin; when you are on your beds, search your hearts and be silent.

Psalm 46:10 — Be still, and know that I am God.

3. We can study with our *minds* (to learn about and give our attention to God).

Ezra 7:10 — Ezra had devoted himself to the study and observance of the Law of the LORD.

Psalm 1:2 — His delight is in the law of the LORD, and on his law he meditates day and night.

2 Corinthians 10:5 — We take captive every thought to make it obedient to Christ.

Author Gary Chapman introduced Christians to a practical concept of love in his classic book *The Five Love Languages*. Chapman says that all people are unique in how they express love and also in how they receive it. Some of us enjoy a loving *touch* (such as a hug or a backrub) as an expression of love, but other people will much prefer hearing some kind *words* over a back rub. *Gifts* are powerful expressions of love to some, but *quality time* outweighs gifts for others. One other segment of humanity doesn't prefer any of the above — what rings their chimes are *deeds of service*.

Chapman's thesis is that we each need to know two things: what our own "love language" is (how we receive and respond to others' loving attempts) and, more important, what love language is in the heart of a person we are trying to love! For example, you may love backrubs yourself, but if your child (or parent, spouse, or friend) loves gifts, your backrub will not count as a gift. It will likely be regarded as more of an annoyance than an expression of love.

Your flight instructor wants to know: *what is God's love*

language? Surely it is all five, so that you can unleash a flurry of loving expressions to Him.

Learning Exercise: God's Love Languages—how can you express each one to God? (Write your thoughts below):

WORDS _____

GIFTS _____

DEEDS_____

QUALITY TIME_____

TOUCH_____

Okay, I admit that "touching" God is rather difficult. But Jesus once said, "Whatever you did for one of the least of these brothers of mine, you did for me" (Matthew 25:40). At the right time, when you give an appropriate and loving touch to a person who needs it (a hand on the shoulder, or even a hug), you will be loving that person in a way that also loves God.

What about this business of loving your neighbor? Exactly who is your neighbor, anyway? Is it the mean guy that lives next door? Is it the driver in the car behind you? Is it Mr. Rogers from public television? In biblical thought, the term *neighbor* is not a term used in covenants (contracts or partnerships) or for marriage, business, or family. *Neighbor* does not refer to anyone with whom you are in any kind of relationship by blood or marriage or political responsibility. But *neighbor* is not the same thing as "stranger" or "enemy." It carries the idea of someone to whom you have no obligation but with whom you do have some contact. The story Jesus used to define *neighbor* is known as the parable of the good Samaritan. It is a story that Jesus told to the man who asked the earlier question about the greatest commandment. After Jesus gave him the answer about loving God and your neighbor, the man asked, "And who is my neighbor?" (Luke 10:29). Right there Jesus told the parable that has become a household expression in our modern language. The story has a greater impact when you know the meaning of the titles given the men in the story, so the terms are explained in the brackets.

According to Luke 10:30-37,

> In reply Jesus said: "A man was going down from Jerusalem to Jericho, when he fell into the hands of robbers. They stripped him of his clothes, beat him and went away, leaving

him half dead. A priest [a Jewish spiritual leader] happened to be going down the same road, and when he saw the man, he passed by on the other side. So too, a Levite, [another Jewish leader, a church worker] when he came to the place and saw him, passed by on the other side. But a Samaritan, [a member of an ethnic group despised by the Jews] as he traveled, came where the man was; and when he saw him, he took pity on him. He went to him and bandaged his wounds, pouring on oil and wine. Then he put the man on his own donkey, took him to an inn and took care of him. The next day he took out two silver coins and gave them to the innkeeper. 'Look after him,' he said, 'and when I return, I will reimburse you for any extra expense you may have.'

"Which of these three do you think was a neighbor to the man who fell into the hands of robbers?" The expert in the law replied, "The one who had mercy on him."

Jesus told him, "Go and do likewise."

This parable really drove home its point by having the hero of the story be a member of an ethnic group despised by the Jews. The "expert in the law" (whose name is mercifully omitted from Scripture) must have blushed when he gave Jesus that final answer.

A modern-day version might sound like this: A man was travelling through America when his car ran into the ditch. A Catholic priest came by, but he didn't want to get involved. An evangelical preacher saw the car in the ditch, but that preacher was late to a planning meeting on community outreach, so he didn't stop. A Middle Easterner, a Muslim, who worked in a convenience store, then passed by, saw the man, and helped him. Yes, Jesus' story had that kind of racial impact on the people of his day.

Let's conclude by saying this: when you come in contact with someone in need, whether by personal encounter, or by reading an article, or hearing a story, can you be ready, willing, and able to help that person? Sometimes the prompting of the Spirit may be, *Do not get involved in this.* (For example, not all believers need to be picking up hitchhikers, or giving money to homeless guys on street corners. Some can; others are not called to do it.)

Twelve years ago, I became aware of the problem of AIDS orphans in Africa, but honestly, I was not doing anything to help. What could I do to help hundreds of thousands, perhaps millions, of kids in lands far away from me? Then, a missionary came to our church and presented the opportunity of sponsoring children through her orphanage. She told of one little six-year-old boy named Duchu Nelson who had lost both parents to AIDS and was living on the farm of an uncle who happened to be a kind of witch doctor. The uncle was willing to feed and house young Nelson, but he did not have the resources to pay either his school fees or his clinic fees. The boy seemed doomed to a life of servitude on that farm, except that in the moment that the missionary told me about him, God prompted me to realize that Duchu Nelson was now my neighbor! I had to take some action to help. I had to do something.

The missionary was operating a sponsorship program, so we signed up to send a small amount of money each month to the orphanage. They used those funds to pay the school and clinic fees and give the uncle a little for groceries. They worked with the uncle to see that the boy was doing as well as possible at home. Twelve years later, Duchu Nelson is a high-school graduate preparing for Christian ministry. We have corresponded over the years through short letters, and recently, he sent me an e-mail! Just think—the poorest six-year-old orphan you can imagine, way out in the African bush, is now a part of the global community. He'll soon do amazing things, because of the power of God to make neighbors out of strangers.

We've covered loving God and loving neighbors, but what about this idea of loving yourself? Doesn't that sound fleshly, or selfish? Certainly it could be, but remember, Jesus said to "love your neighbor as yourself," so He is equating those two at some level. Jesus is calling us to love and respect ourselves in a uniquely healthy way. You can learn to see yourself as a spiritual being, created by God and redeemed by the Savior, and that self-image is accurate. This is quite different from loving your own flesh nature and allowing it to dominate your spiritual nature. What Jesus wants is for us to see every other person we encounter as also a spiritual being created in the image of God. The author C. S. Lewis, in *The Weight of Glory*, said, "There are no ordinary people. You have never met a mere mortal."

Learning Exercise: Read Psalm 139, and ponder these five principles of good self-esteem. [Source: Bible study by Pastor Emeritus Jimmy Smith of Bear Valley Church, Lakewood, Colorado]

Psalm 139 (Select and write one phrase that impacts you the most.)

1. Go to the right source — God. (vv. 1–6)

_____

2. View yourself as God's special creation. (vv. 7–12)

_____

3. Affirm the wonderfulness of it. (vv. 13–16)

_____

4. Accept the authority of God's Word. (vv. 17–18)

_____

5. Realize God's concern for you. (vv. 23–24)

_____

THE FOUR FORCES OF LOVE

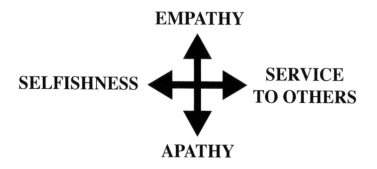

EMPATHY

SELFISHNESS ←→ SERVICE TO OTHERS

APATHY

The lifting power of love is well documented in the famous "love chapter" of the Bible, 1 Corinthians 13. The core verses are 4–7: "Love is patient, love is kind. It does not envy, it does not boast, it is not proud. It is not rude, it is not self-seeking, it is not easily angered, it keeps no record of wrongs. Love does not delight in evil but rejoices with the truth. It always protects, always trusts, always hopes, always perseveres."

Apathy (or indifference) will weigh down anyone's ability to love. Speaking of the coming last days, Jesus said, "At that time many will turn away from the faith and will betray and hate each other, and many false prophets will appear and deceive many people. Because of the increase of wickedness, the love of most will grow cold" (Matthew 24:10–12).

"Carry each other's burdens, and in this way you will fulfill the law of Christ." Service to others, according to Galatians 6:2, is a fulfillment of the law of Christ (the Great Commandment). This requires us to overcome selfishness, as per the command in Romans 15:1: "We who are strong ought to bear with the failings of the weak and not to please ourselves."

Chapter Ten Quiz

1. God wants us to love all of these except:
    a) our neighbor
    b) our enemy
    c) our possessions

2. Which one of these is not a *love language*?
    a) touch
    b) deed of service
    c) advice
    d) quality time

3. The person who would be your neighbor is:
    a) someone who lives near you
    b) someone who works with you
    c) someone you play sports with
    d) all of the above

4. The part of your self that God wants you to love is:
    a) the fleshly part with all of its appetites
    b) the redeemed part with its spiritual awareness

5. Loving your enemies means:
    a) you pray for them, for God to bless and redeem them
    b) you pray against them, for God to destroy them
    c) you pray that God will grant you victory over them

6. The classic chapter in the Bible on love is:
   a) John 3
   b) Romans 8
   c) 1 Corinthians 13
   d) Revelation 20

7. An emotional vice that seems to be the very opposite of love is:
   a) anger
   b) depression
   c) apathy
   d) lust

8. When Jesus gave the "greatest commandment," He was quoting from:
   a) Genesis
   b) Exodus
   c) Psalms
   d) Deuteronomy

9. Jesus said caring for which of these people would be like caring for Him?
   a) the greatest among you
   b) the worst among you
   c) the least among you
   d) the best among you

10. What made the good Samaritan parable so shocking is the hero who was identified as a:
   a) Levite
   b) Priest
   c) Samaritan
   d) Roman

Questions for Group Discussion

Get to know others on the flight:
Have you ever been beside the road in need of help?

Have you ever been the Samaritan who stopped to help?

What were these experiences like for you?

Flying higher:
Describe a moment when you felt truly loved by a person. If you can, list five such times.

Thank God for these. Consider how they are similar or different.

Describe a moment when you felt unloved. If you can, make another list of five. Thank God that He loves you all the time. Consider how they are similar or not.

Are you someone who receives love easily, or do you resist being loved by others? Why do you think this is true? Would you rather give or receive love?

Let your imagination take flight:
Brennan Manning describes being so excited to see someone that he literally jumped up and down with joy. Can you envision Jesus being this excited to see you in heaven?

How do you envision your entry into heaven?

Quiz answers: 1c, 2c, 3d, 4b, 5a, 6c, 7c, 8d, 9c, 10c

At last, you have completed your study of *When Faith Takes Flight*. Now you are ready to go solo—I believe in you! You have reviewed and passed the quizzes on ten very important topics of the Christian life. Now go forth, and put faith to your spiritual flight!

Please feel welcome to visit the author's website: www.whenfaithtakesflight.com.

Where Eagles Fly

Lord of the heavens and Lord of the skies,
Teach me the things that Eagles do,
So I may go where the Eagle flies,
And pierce the veil of splendid blue.

Lord, give me the wisdom and strong resolve,
To master the art of soaring flight
And tame the winds of the Earth's revolve,
So I may drift through the starlight night.

Lord, give me the courage, that I may dare
To slip and turn and roll with glee,
And to visit once the Eagle's lair,
So through your grace, I am set free.

Lord, touch my soul, and capture my heart,
Come fly with me when I'm alone,
May we soar together, and never apart,
And dance the skies, where Eagles roam.

Let me not forget, or doubt your power,
O Lord of the heavens and Lord of the skies,
Who created the heights where Eagles tower,
So I may go where the Eagle flies.

Alas I see a landing place
You've saved for me a nest that's safe
So I may rest, and say goodbye,
To the realm of space, where Eagles fly.

Bruce Dean Oaster
Christmas Eve, 2007

Recommended Reading

Alcorn, Randy. *The Treasure Principle*. Sisters, OR: Multnomah, 2001.

Bailey, Faith. *George Mueller: He Dared to Trust God for the Needs of Countless Orphans*. Chicago: Moody Bible Institute, 1958.

Bainton, Roland. *Here I Stand: A Life of Martin Luther*. New York: Abingdon-Cokesbury, 1950.

Chapman, Gary. *The Five Love Languages*. Chicago: Northfield, 1992.

Chase, Marry Ellen. *The Lovely Ambition*. New York: W. W. Norton, 1960.

Dean, Jennifer Kennedy *The Praying Life: Living Beyond Your Limits*. Birmingham: New Hope, 1993.

Hallock, Edgar Francis. *Preacher Hallock: All the Promises*. Eugene, OR: Wipf and Stock, 2006.

Hybels, Bill. *Too Busy Not to Pray: Slowing Down to Be with God*. Downers Grove, IL: InterVarsity, 1988.

Lewis, C. S. *Mere Christianity*. New York: Harper, 2001.

Manning, Brennan. *The Ragamuffin Gospel: Good News for the Bedraggled, Beat-Up, and Burnt Out.* Portland: Multnomah, 1990.

Mears, Henrietta. *What the Bible Is All About.* Ventura, CA: Regal, 1983.

Powell, Diane Hennacy. *The ESP Enigma: The Scientific Case for Psychic Phenomena.* New York: Walker, 2009.

Rinker, Rosalyn. *Conversational Prayer.* Waco, TX: Word, 1984.

Shelley, Bruce. *Church History in Plain Language.* Dallas: Word, 1982.

Seton, Ernest Thompson. *Gospel of the Red Man.* New York: Doubleday Doran, 1936

Stroebel, Lee. *The Case for Christ: A Journalist's Personal Investigation of the Evidence for Jesus.* Grand Rapids: Zondervan, 1998.

Swindoll, Charles. *The Grace Awakening.* Dallas: Word, 1990.

Warren, Rick. *The Purpose-Driven Life: What on Earth Am I Here For?* Grand Rapids: Zondervan, 2002.

ABOUT THE AUTHOR

Jim Walters serves as senior pastor of Bear Valley Church in Lakewood, Colorado. He grew up at the Robert Mueller airport in Austin, Texas, where his father worked as an air traffic controller and flight instructor. When Jim was a sixteen-year-old high-school student, he was carefully taught to fly, by his father.

Jim became a flight instructor while completing a business degree at the University of Texas at Austin. In 1972, he completed pilot training in the Air Force and was deployed to Southeast Asia in an F-4 Phantom fighter jet, just as the Vietnam War ended. Later he was an instructor pilot at the Air Force pilot school in Lubbock, Texas.

After a move to Dallas, Texas, Jim served on the staff of International Commission, a partnership missions agency, and at Casa View Baptist Church. Since 1995, he has been at Bear Valley Church in Lakewood, Colorado. He holds a master of divinity degree from Southwestern Baptist Theological Seminary. He is an Eagle Scout and is active in the Scouting movement. He and his wife, Connie, have two grown daughters, Wendy and Bethie.

Visit the author's website: www.whenfaithtakesflight.com

- Take the 100-question Basic Bible Knowledge Exams.
- Post a comment about this book.
- E-mail the author with questions or stories.
- Follow the blog and request the free e-newsletter.
- Inquire about volume discounts: jim@whenfaithtakesflight.com
- Sign up for prerelease notifications for volume 2, *Faith Flying Higher*.

Reorder this book by credit card at the website or by check for the full cover price (free shipping) payable to:

Go Victor Sales
9956 W. Remington Place #A-10 Suite 238
Littleton, CO 80128

ALSO BY JIM WALTERS:

Practical e-books on raising finances for ministry:

Raising Support for Missions Trips
Raising Support as a Church Planter
Upgrading Missionary Support Letters
Planning and Financing a House Church
Reaching Multi-family Housing Residents
Steps for Starting a New 501(c)3 Ministry

These e-books are available at www.missionfundraising.com

Intermedia Publishing Group

Publishing That Works For You

Do you need a speaker?

Do you want Jim Walters to speak to your group or event? Then contact Larry Davis at: (623) 337-8710 or email: ldavis@intermediapr.com or use the contact form at: www.intermediapr.com.

Whether you want to purchase bulk copies of *When Faith Takes Flight* or buy another book for a friend, get it now at: www.imprbooks.com.

If you have a book that you would like to publish, contact Terry Whalin, Publisher, at Intermedia Publishing Group, (623) 337-8710 or email: twhalin@intermediapub.com or use the contact form at: www.intermediapub.com.